Praise for "Tropical Attire Encouraged"

Alison Rosen is that TMI friend that tells you everything, the good and bad and, most wonderfully, the ugly. She doesn't mince words and she doesn't bullshit. Just the God's honest truth about her own hilarious insanity.

> — MICHAEL IAN BLACK, actor, comedian, author

Alison has created a hilariously quirky world where you're turning the page because you can't get enough of how funny it is when she talks about things she is NOT doing—like going to parties, buying age-appropriate jeans, using the phone, or wearing underwear. A day inside Alison's head for fellow neurotics is our version of a day at the beach.

> — JEN KIRKMAN, New York Times best-selling author of *"I Can Barely Take Care of Myself,"* star of Netflix original comedy specials *"I'm Gonna Die Alone (and I Feel Fine)"* and *"Just Keep Livin'?"*

This book is more fun than a Tiki party. A lot more fun. Alison Rosen is hilarious when talking about everything from melon ballers to feminism, from dog neutering to wedding planning. Reading the book feels like having dinner with your most fun friend—though one who might not remember your name (see column "I Can't Remember Your Name").

> — A.J. JACOBS, four-time New York Times best-selling author, journalist, editor at *Esquire*, *NPR* commentator, lecturer

Hilarious, introspective, and makes you feel like you aren't the craziest person you know. Thank you Alison for reminding me why you are one of the few people I don't hate.

> — SHANE DAWSON, *YouTuber*, podcaster, author

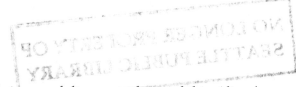
If you're struggling with being an adult, you need to read this. Alison's stories are a good reminder that you don't always have to be. ... Plus it's way funnier when you're not.

— SARAH COLONNA, New York Times best-selling author of *"Life As I Blow It,"* comedian, former writer on *"Chelsea Lately"*

From the moment I met her, I felt Alison Rosen would be my "New Best Friend." Now that I know what a talented writer she is, she is def going on my list of enemies.

— JENNY MOLLEN, New York Times best-selling author of *"I Like You Just the Way I Am"* and *"Live Fast Die Hot,"* actress

Women seeking an honest and funny friend will be as satisfied with Alison's book as men who are trying to understand them.

— GREG FITZSIMMONS, stand-up comedian, television writer and producer, *SiriusXM* host

Alison Rosen has an extremely sharp sense of what's funny about both herself and the world around her. She writes with wit, compassion, and exuberance that make every page a treat!

— JOSH GONDELMAN, writer on *"Last Week Tonight With John Oliver,"* comedian

Being in Alison Rosen's mind is funny and exhausting. How she gets out of bed every day astounds me. Then again, you don't have to get out of bed to write.

— JOEL STEIN, writer, journalist

Alison's slightly obsessive self-exploration is enlightening, comforting and deeply funny all at once. If she wasn't already your New Best Friend, she'll undoubtedly be by the end of this breezy read.

— MOLLY MCALEER, host of *"Plz Advise"* podcast, co-founder of *HelloGiggles*

Tropical Attire Encouraged
(and Other Phrases That Scare Me)

Alison Rosen

Creators Publishing
Hermosa Beach, CA

Cover art by Randi Lawson
Interior illustrations by Daniel Quantz
Creative coordinator Peter Kaminski

CREATORS PUBLISHING
737 3rd St
Hermosa Beach, CA 90254
310-337-7003

The events and conversations in this book have been recreated from the author's memory to the best of her ability.

Library of Congress Control Number: 2017935746
ISBN (e-book): 978-1-945630-34-7
ISBN (print): 978-1-945630-35-4

First Edition

Printed in the United States of America
1 3 5 7 9 10 8 6 4

For my family

Contents

The Gift Certificate

I've misplaced a gift certificate to a jewelry store I don't like, and it's driving me insane. It's only for about $31—not even enough to buy a necklace I don't want—and yet the fact that at one point I had it and now I don't is unacceptable. I want to have my cake and eat it, too. But I don't want to eat it; I just want to know it's there. Granted, it's a cake I don't like—probably something atrocious with gumballs in it—but it's my disgusting cake, and I will rip this house apart until I find it.

Part of the problem is this scrap of paper has zigzagged across the country with me for the last four years. I've forged a relationship with it, not unlike the one I have with the empty lipstick tubes rolling around my dresser, which turn it into a giant clattering maraca. I've been hanging on to them for years because any day now, I may take advantage of the store's eco incentive of a free lipstick of your choice in exchange for empty tubes. Do you know how many times I've walked past this store wanting to buy lipstick but unable because it seems foolish to pay for something I could get for free?

Once, when I had the kind of time on my hands that unemployment affords, I actually did bring the tubes with me to the store with the intention of trading them in.

"I would like a free lipstick!" I announced victoriously, pushing my greasy booty toward the clerk in a Ziploc bag. But there were so many choices! Matte, frost, crème, reds, browns, peaches, maroons, pinks, purples. Of course, I could just buy—correction, choose—my regular, but that would be so boring. This was an opportunity to shake things up! A chance to color outside the lines.

After smearing a crayon box's worth of samples on the back of my hands and then trying unsuccessfully to wipe it all off with a tissue, I realized I'd been foolhardy in thinking I could casually make this decision. Plus, I was told that at a different location you could exchange the tubes for a free eye shadow. Maybe that was what I really wanted. As an indecisive control freak who's always sure there's something better around the corner, all my lesser qualities had come together at once to leave me paralyzed.

Clearly, I should just march right into my bedroom and open up that drawer and throw out all those empty tubes that I'm never going to exchange. They are taking up space, making me feel like a protohoarder and making it impossible for me to buy lipstick without guilt. My luscious pout deserves better! I'm totally going to free myself of these crimson shackles ... right after I find the gift certificate.

Oh, God. What if the jewelry store—a pretentious little boutique that sells yoga-inspired charms and doesn't accept returns, which is how I got into this mess to begin with (I exchanged a gift I didn't want for store credit. Quit judging me.)— goes out of business before I've had a chance to remind myself that there's nothing I want there?

I'm pretty sure the slip is either tucked into a book for safekeeping or sitting in the pocket of a handbag. I can definitely remember putting it in one of those places. Unfortunately, I can remember each action with equal vividness, which is causing me to regard my own memory in the same circumspect way you view an insincere friend who looooooooves your new hairdo.

Clearly, I've left myself no choice but to open and shake every single book I own, including the self-help ones whose spines face the wall, lest a potential suitor stop by unannounced. Granted, turning the spines against the wall paints a potentially worse portrait, one that suggests I don't know how to use a bookshelf. But these are the risks you take, and it's not as if I have any available dresser drawer space.

"Oh, you're reading 'What Your Doctor Isn't Telling You About Your Abnormal Pap Smear'? I must have you right now, you sexy minx!" I can't imagine anyone ever saying. Or, "Yes, of course I don't mind if you slip into something more comfortable. I'll just be here, thinking of you and flipping through this well-worn copy of 'I Hate You, Don't Leave Me.' Oh, how cute. You highlighted it. What's that sound? Are you popping popcorn in your dresser?"

Incidentally, "I Hate You, Don't Leave Me" is how I feel about the gift certificate, which is why I have to find it—so I can purge my environment of this toxin once and for all!

Or slip it into my copy of "Clutter's Last Stand: It's Time To De-Junk Your Life."

ooo

Is Adulthood an Illusion?

T he other day, while simultaneously plucking gray hairs and applying zit cream, it occurred to me that I don't really feel like an adult, not in the ways I would have expected.

It's not exactly that I feel young. I no longer possess the desire to stay out all hours, the urge to change the world or the patience to talk on the phone—those were beaten out of me years ago. And it's not like I feel fresh-faced, dewy, supple or elastic—my window to have a perfect bikini body closed before it opened, and sometimes my back hurts if I sit in one position for too long. But in terms of things like knowing what to do if my car breaks down, feeling comfortable calling my friends' parents by their first names, an ease with making small talk at dinner parties, fearlessness—you know, the big-ticket adult items—I'm woefully bereft.

By my age, my mom had two kids and had put both parents in the ground. I just adopted a puppy, which feels like a huge, scary commitment, and my insurmountable task for the day is to figure out how to return the bra I bought online because somehow having to pack it back up in the box and then put the right amount of postage on it and find a mailbox seems like a real pain in the butt.

Maybe I'll just keep it and hope my chest grows.

Knowing how to purchase a properly fitting bra, according to my mother, is not only something I should have mastered by my age but also a goal and a reward in itself.

"You need to have someone size you," she'll admonish. "The correct fit makes a world of difference, and it's much more comfortable!"

I believe her, sort of, but the idea of having a matronly bra specialist get up in my business with a tape measure and various other tools of the trade (A variety of domed objects, from melon baller to salad bowl? I have no idea what goes on there.) doesn't sound fun at all. It sounds like a gynecologist visit. Speaking of, crap, I need to schedule one of those. So instead of availing myself to a pro, I'll continue to make the error of blindly purchasing something that could support a couple oranges for what are more like tangerines.

But the more I talk to my friends, some of whom have ill-fitting bras, some of whom don't—I don't discriminate—the more I realize we all feel this way. None of us learned how to be a grown-up.

Is it technology that's made us so dependent? I no longer know anyone's phone numbers because they're stored in my phone, which really should be called my "text," as that's all I do with it. The notion of trying to schedule lunch with someone who doesn't text or email causes me panic. Remember when people used to make plans by calling you on the phone and asking you questions in real time, which you then had to answer in real time while the other person sat there, breathing into a dumbbell-shaped receiver that was some beige or white monstrosity attached to the base on the wall by a big tangled squiggle of a cord? The only benefit of said cord was it provided you with something to do with your hands while being interrogated. But here's the diabolical genius of the cord: No matter how many times you untangled it, by either dramatically yanking the double helix apart as if showing that piece of rubber who's boss or wrapping it around your fingers and possibly cutting off your circulation in an effort to coax it back into shape, it snapped right back into a tangled mess the minute you turned your back. Left to its own devices, I'm pretty sure it would turn into a dreadlock.

But maybe it's overly simplistic to blame our growing almost-an-adultness on technology, especially when I took a poll of adults over 30 recently and asked them what age they feel inside and the answers ranged from 4 to 23.

Have we all been hoodwinked into buying into this idea that there will be a point at which we feel fully formed? Is adulthood an illusion? I think I expected that one day I would magically be a grown-up and a certain confidence, wisdom and fearlessness would be conferred upon me, as if the more candles I blew out, the less I'd second-guess myself. Do you know how often I walk away from an exchange feeling like it went exactly as I'd hoped and I left a stellar impression?

Yesterday, I tried to exit a co-worker's car with my seat belt still fastened. Embarrassed to find myself still in the seat, trapped like a turtle on its back, I undid the belt and stood up only to launch my cellphone, which had been loose on my lap, into the gutter.

That's the kind of suavity I'm working with.

But if you think this means I'll be using any sort of landline to conduct my affairs, you're sorely mistaken.

Better go email my mom to ask for advice.

ooo

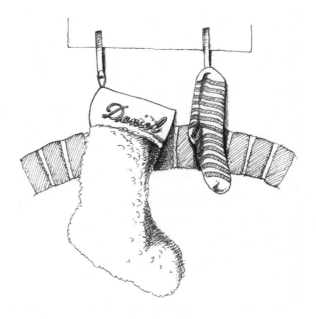

The Impending Chrismapolypse

When I was little, I vowed not to become one of those people who dreads the holidays. One of those people, like my parents, who grimaces at the sound of Bing Crosby and grumbles at the sight of dirigible Santas and oversized candy canes being inflated on rooftops in October; and who seems to age many years over the course of one gift-buying season. The notion of being relieved that the holidays are over was as foreign to me as disliking "Sesame Street" or liking cilantro. My little brain just couldn't make sense of it.

Instead, I loved every part of the season, from the advent calendars with their waxy chocolate, to the glittery crafts and dried macaroni wreaths coated in gold paint, to the sappy songs we'd memorize for the school pageant—an event held in the gymnasium at night. Just seeing a place at night I'd only ever seen during the daytime was thrilling enough. But factor in the tights, patent leather shoes, clip-on earrings and blue eye shadow my mom let me wear—accouterments fit for a 1940s stripper—and I felt like I'd won some kind of yuletide lottery.

The excitement only intensified as the big day drew near. I was like a tiny holiday crack addict, and each successive sight and smell was another electrifying dose. Eggnog? YES, PLEASE. Tinsel? I LOVE TINSEL. Christmas cookies? MUST. EAT. COOKIES. Fake snow? YESSSSSS. Picture with Santa? YES. Not even sitting on the lap of a sweaty, handsy alcoholic in itchy polyester could dampen my spirits.

By the time promos for "How the Grinch Stole Christmas" and "Frosty the Snowman" came on TV, I had butterflies in my stomach and was short of breath. How I'd ever get to sleep on Christmas Eve was beyond me.

But somehow (slowly, impossibly) the time would pass, and by about 4:30 or 5 a.m. I'd wake up and then force myself to stay in bed for as long as possible—another 15 minutes tops. When I could no longer take it, I'd scramble out of bed, grab the stockings from the living room and wake up my little sister, and we'd sit in bed reading magazines and eating candy and playing with our collectible holiday pencils. It was a bunch of crap—under the tree was where the real treasures lay—but we loved it.

At some point I lost the holiday spirit in a very big way. I'm not sure when or why, but I'm now that grumpy adult I never wanted to be, counting down the minutes until this ridiculously ornate pine-scented charade is over and real life can resume. What's that you say? You finished all your shopping early? I hate you in a very real, very frightening, white-hot burning, all caps kind of way. HATE.

I still enjoy the songs (sort of) and the treats (although I fear the calories), but mostly I just feel enervated by the expectations and the crowds and the forced merriment. My boyfriend is the keeper of the holiday spirit in our house, and if it weren't for him, I don't know that we would have gotten a tree. Going out into the cold and selecting one, tying it to the roof of the car, dragging it up the steps, getting needles everywhere and then having to deal with the hassle of getting rid of it a few weeks later just seems like a pain. And I don't know that I would do the whole gift exchange. Battling the crowds and paying top dollar for something that will go on sale one day after Christmas, not even knowing whether what you're buying is what the person wants, and wrapping and measuring and cutting and taping and tying bows and making out cards all seems like a pain. And the dinner with all the dirty dishes and the parties with the mind-numbing, soul-deadening small talk? No, thank you.

But I hate that I feel this way, and I hate that I wish I could climb into bed and hide until mid-January.

I'm trying my hardest to snap out of it so at least I don't bring others down to my level. But underneath it all, I desperately wish I could feel the happiness and excitement I felt as a kid.

Am I alone with my spiritual stocking full of coal?

Let me know how you're feeling about the impending Chrismapolypse and what you're doing to cope. Maybe we can pool survival strategies and get through it together. (Unless you're the type who finished all your shopping months ago because you do it year-round. You'll just make the rest of us feel bad.)

ooo

Puppy

My boyfriend and I recently brought home a puppy, which means we've said goodbye to sleeping, leaving the house unless it's absolutely necessary, taking a step without looking down, having a home that's decorated with anything other than squeaky rubber toys, the blissful ignorance that comes from not knowing what a bully stick is and owning a remote control with an uneaten No. 4 button—though this is fine because we no longer have the time or attention span to watch TV.

We've also bid adieu to romance for the most part. Yesterday, as Daniel was leaving for work and I was about to get in the shower, he popped his head in, appraised my state of undress—something that formerly would have given him pause—and yelled with the fervor of someone whose sports team won, "He pooped!"

I wish I could say I'd reached similar heights of ecstasy over the dog's bowel function, but I was too busy trying to get out of the shower as fast as humanly possible, for fear of where and in what state I'd find the tiny, adorable beast when I got out.

Have you ever implored the water to come out of the nozzle faster? I feel like I'm suddenly in a race against the clock and everything is conspiring to slow me down. I'm beginning to understand why new mothers opt for no-nonsense hairstyles. I no longer care whether I'm frizz-free, or whether my eyeliner tips up perfectly at the outer corners of my eyes, or whether my clothes are covered in puppy fur. I've accepted that when I walk into a room, people wonder why it smells like Snausages. I have more important things to manage, namely, keeping this helpless attention whore alive.

And that right there, the overwhelming, unrelenting sense of responsibility, is the part I hadn't quite anticipated. Since bringing home this tiny puppy—all ears and paws and wagging tail—that loves to have his belly rubbed, sits on command and also sits when I try to take him for a walk, I feel like there's a pot on the stove about to boil over or, and this may only resonate with some of you, as if I've left my straightening iron plugged in.

At all times, there's a Rolodex of ways he could hurt himself flashing through my mind. Whenever I find that he's fine, curled up in his bed with his head resting on his giraffe toy, I feel like we've narrowly escaped some inevitable misfortune. It's exhausting.

I realize it might seem offensive to suggest the experience of having a new puppy is anywhere close to that of having a new baby. I don't mean to suggest it's the same. I mean to suggest it's worse.

With a baby, you get nine months to prepare. Not only that, you can rely on your maternal or paternal instincts. With a puppy, those instincts kick in, but you have to override them and try to think like a dog instead of a human. This is why I spent the morning rooting through the trash before walking through my food. This afternoon, I plan to eat a Kleenex and then, if things break my way, lick some freshly applied lotion. Depending on my mood, I might whine.

Well-meaning people tried to tell us: "You should get an adult dog. Have you considered an adult dog?" The short answer is we wanted the cuteness of a puppy. The even shorter answer is we were stupid. But as much as I say that I've learned my lesson, I suspect I will be in the same position again someday because the memory of agony is very short but adorable pictures—of which I've taken a million—last forever. So, one day, when I no longer smell like Alpo and have had a full night of sleep, I will probably be foolish enough to think it's a good idea to get anther puppy. If I do, please say no to me in a calm, assertive way.

Now, if you'll excuse me, these zippers aren't going to eat themselves.

ooo

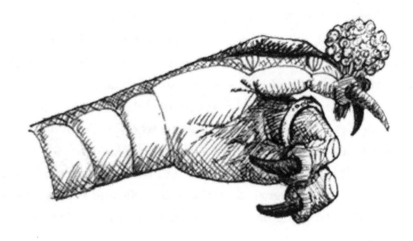

The Soft-Spoken Bridezilla

I f I appear dazed, helpless and possibly in need of medical attention, as if I've just escaped captivity, please forgive me. It's just that I've been talking about weddings with my mother.

I don't mean to sound like an ingrate, and I do love the woman, but she and I have vastly different philosophies on how to spend our time and money.

For example, I like to avoid fruitless missions. She loves them. Or at least it would seem that way, given the nature of most of our conversations regarding the impending nuptials, about which nothing has been decided.

I can't remember her exact words. At a certain point I have to tune out for self-preservation. The gist is always that she was talking to [person I don't know] who [has some very tenuous connection to matrimony] who suggested I do [something that sounds like nothing I want any part of]. Here's an example:

"I was talking to Karen. You remember Karen, right? Oh, you don't? Well, she has a niece who just got married, but her niece's boss's sister, Darlene, has been to tons of weddings. Why don't you call Darlene? I bet she has a lot of wedding ideas!"

Talking to someone who's been to a lot of weddings to get wedding ideas is like talking to someone who's had a lot of surgery to learn how to perform a heart transplant.

And if I seem grave or intense, it's just that I keep panicking when I hear the average wedding costs $28,000 and yet my dream of the perfect wedding has never included the words "BYOB" or "potluck."

Plus, I've just never really enjoyed talking about weddings in general. I'm neither a tomboy nor emotionally dead inside—I love puppies and romantic comedies, and the silliest things make me cry—but I seem to be missing that very girly gene that allows one to brighten at the sight of lace, fall in love with table linens and care whether things are tented or not.

When I was about 4 years old, I had a clear vision of what I thought a wedding was. You'd walk down a long, greenish hallway wearing a white dress, and there would be a line of men in tuxedos from which you'd select your husband. Not only did this vision avoid any wedding planning but I also think I invented "The Bachelorette."

"Enjoy this time of life," more than one of my parents' friends has said in cards they've sent to my fiancé and me. You know who loves weddings more than the bride and groom? Your parents' friends. I didn't even realize getting engaged is cause for a card, but it is. And it's not like they're taking those sad blank cards with the generic images of flowers on the front and writing engagement wishes inside. They are shopping in the engagement card aisle. There are cards intended for this very purpose.

It's making me wish I could do more cherishing and savoring than worrying and grumbling.

The thing is, despite my foul attitude, I'm very much in love with my fiancé, and I'm excited about our life together. This has nothing to do with him and everything to do with the fact that planning a wedding combines three of my least favorite things: planning, making decisions and fashion.

I'm an indecisive person who hates shopping and waits until the very last minute to commit to plans. And yet I don't want to elope. I thought I might as a way to avoid what feels like the world's frilliest scavenger hunt, but the more cards I put up on the refrigerator, the more I think I really do want the big ceremony.

I like things that are lovely and nice and beautiful. I just don't know how to make them that way. And while I don't want to be involved in every decision, I also don't really trust anyone else to make the decisions for me.

I just had an awful realization: I'm a bridezilla.

I'm a soft-spoken, indecisive bridezilla who makes fart jokes and seems easygoing but is secretly a tyrant.

Given this unpleasant revelation, I'd like to go ahead and apologize preemptively to everyone around me, including my parents, siblings, friends, parents' friends, co-workers, fiancé and fiancé's family. And I may as well apologize to you, too, because I fear I may have to drag you along with me like tiny wedding hostages. If it's any consolation, the maid of honor is making her fantastic macaroni and cheese.

Could you bring napkins and ice?

ooo

Kids, Dogs and Puppies

Walking a puppy is a lot like walking a Kardashian. You can't go very fast; strangers stop you repeatedly; and the conversation isn't very stimulating.

In the case of the puppy, this is how it goes down. From a short distance, approaching strangers will slow to a standstill and begin to *ooh* and *aah*.

There will be nudging and pointing followed by some debate about whether they're looking at a puppy or just a small, uncoordinated dog. Perhaps they've been burned before.

By the time they've determined it is indeed a puppy, the initial spotter will have made sure all members of the party—spouses, children, dogs—are aware of the approaching visitor.

One woman cooed to her disinterested puggle: "See the baby? Do you see the baby? Look, Riley, a baby!"

Poor Riley wanted to continue his walk, but his owner didn't get it. It was like watching someone repeatedly say to a carrot: "Look, carrot! A baby carrot!" and expect to get a reaction.

This notion that dogs would be anywhere near as excited as we are by smaller, younger, less well-behaved versions of themselves is a curious one.

Children, on the other hand, do have a reaction: fear.

More than once, I've felt like a guilty accomplice when parents invite the bouncy, adorable, uncontrolled ball of energy on the other end of the leash to terrorize their children. They mistakenly assume their kids are having the same OH. MY. GOD. SO. CUTE. SO. LITTLE. MUST. SNUGGLE. PUPPY. NOW. GIVE. ME. THAT. PUPPY!!!! reaction they're having, so they're always confused when their kids become distraught or pull away.

It's a matter of scale, of course. And what's silly, floppy and no bigger than a desert boot to us is much larger, scarier and unpredictable to a child.

Plus, what we find irresistible and fun doesn't always translate, which is why I'm still angry at my mom for surprising me with a clown at my sixth birthday party. Did she intend to consign me to a lifetime of bozophobia? Just thinking about JoJo's weird red yarn hair—the equivalent of clown cornrows—and oversized rubber shoes is enough to make me sweat.

But back to the streets.

Here's the thing about the way kids and dogs react: I think they might be right. *We're* the ones who are so distracted by cuteness that we're willing to forgive everything else. Kids and dogs look past the pleading eyes and wagging tail into the dark heart of the beast.

Do I think my puppy is out to get me? Of course not, but he'd gladly knife me for some string cheese if his paws could work a blade.

I'm not saying he's evil. He's just out for himself, like a reality show contestant or someone who loves "The Fountainhead."

But that thing where he walks through his food and then jumps in your lap and puts his messy paws on your face? I'm pretty sure that's the dog equivalent of waiting until you pass out at a party to write on your face with a Sharpie.

And then there are the times when he bites the Ottoman while looking up at you when he wants attention; or plays a version of fetch where you end up throwing *and* retrieving the toy; or gets a sudden surge of energy when he manages to snag something that isn't his, as if he were Pac-Man and a dirty sock were a power pellet.

Actually, maybe he really is evil. But not in an invade Poland kind of way—more in a "Jackass" kind of way. He's like a misbehaving drunk teenager. Or Lindsay Lohan—he gets away with his shenanigans because he's so cute and was in "Herbie: Fully Loaded." Plus, it's always possible he just doesn't know any better.

These are the options: He's either a good-natured simpleton or a manipulative genius that loves cheese. When he finds and pulls all the stuffed squirrels out of his puzzle toy, I think he's a genius. When he shoves his head inside the toy and gets stuck and walks into furniture, I'm less sure.

I should give him a drug test just to be safe.

ooo

His, Mine and Ours

I recently did something very loving, tender, romantic and kind-hearted. I walked from room to room in the apartment I share with my fiancé, trying to figure out who's ruined more of whose stuff.

It started innocently enough. One afternoon, he announced it was time to purchase new blue jeans.

Like so many of us, he'd been wearing the same few pairs long enough that they'd become comfortable, which is nature's way of telling you they're no longer in style.

The following morning, he waltzed out the door in soft, faded Levi's and then returned in supersaturated dark-blue skinny jeans, struggling to move.

"I'm a skinny jeans guy now!" he declared, teetering.

He hobbled to the couch and then fell on it. This is how he sits now.

I didn't think much of it. If he wants to muffin-top his ankles, that's his business. But then I started noticing something strange: Half of our—and by "our" I mean "my"—beige couch was turning gray.

At first I assumed it was some weird, butt-shaped shadow. But the more I inspected it, the more I realized the dark cloud was on the fabric itself.

I struggled to identify the culprit. Newsprint? Cigar smoke? Soot?

Had someone been entertaining an erudite cigar-smoking chimney sweep behind my back? It seemed unlikely.

But then I heard my beloved gasping for breath from the other room.

Of course! His jeans were leaking!

I informed Skinny Jeans that his new personality was leaving a mark all over my—I mean "our"—furniture and that he might want to consider dropping the new duds in the wash.

A look of panic flashed across his face.

I felt bad because I knew I was asking him to risk shrinkage, which would mean him having to wake up a good 60 minutes earlier to get dressed. But as far as I could tell, we only had two options: Shrink the skinny jeans, or invite The California Raisins over to rub themselves on the couch to even out the tone.

Then I began to wonder whether he was wiping his blue butt all over my couch in retaliation for crimes I'd committed against his pillowcases early in our relationship.

Allow me to explain.

I am a grown woman in many ways—age being the main one—but I still have the skin of a teenager. (Her name was Cheryl.) Because I still break out, I often slather on acne cream before bed, which works to control and cure breakouts, repel the opposite sex and bleach the bejesus out of any fabric with which it comes in contact.

I learned this the hard way, when Daniel asked why his eyes burned when he hugged me and why his blue pillowcases were streaked with orange.

I went on to destroy his blue face towels and white bath sheets with mascara and lipstick.

I also damaged his vacuum. While vacuuming, I went around a corner, which accidentally yanked the cord from the wall and bent the prongs. And the plastic.

But who's really keeping track? I mean, aside from me.

The vacuum had it coming because it beguiled me with its "handy" wand attachment, which is coiled and stuffed into the back of the vacuum, ready to strike. I had no idea that if I released the wand from its holster, I would not only suddenly feel as if I were battling an angry robot but also never be able to stuff it back into the machine without first learning origami. It's right up there with cheap horizontal blinds in terms of flimsy pieces of plastic with a deeply ingrained sense of individualism.

So, one could say we're even. And yet, I still think the couch offense is bigger, simply because the couch is larger. And because it's mine.

I'm left with two questions: At what point will I stop thinking of our belongings as his or mine and just think of them as ours? And if I rub my face on his skinny jeans, will I bleach his jeans or turn my face blue?

I'm going to find out. Worst-case scenario I'll become a chimney sweep.

ooo

The Fearlessness of Youth (and Puppies)

My fiancé's least favorite part of walking our new puppy, Oliver, isn't tripping over the leash, carrying around a bag of hot poop or trying to stop him from putting anything and everything—including cigarette butts, snails and dirt clods—into his little mouth. It's when strangers ask him what the puppy's name is. Daniel is hesitant to answer, as he worries it might somehow lead to Oliver being dognapped.

I think it's cute he's under the impression Oliver knows his own name.

Because I am a woman of science, and because I'm a little bored, I tested my theory that Oliver would answer to basically any name if it were delivered in an enthusiastic, chirpy, I-may-or-may-not-have-a-treat-for-you tone of voice—the tone of voice you'd use when praising a 5-year-old or a very drunk 25-year-old for tying his shoes.

As predicted, Oliver responded to each of the "Top 10 Hottest Baby Names of 2013"—even Mavis.

And while I am in favor of Daniel's protective instinct, I'm unclear how knowing Oliver's name would make it easier to dognap him. It's not as if Oliver's in the habit of demanding a name. He's little and sometimes annoying, but other than that he's nothing like Rumpelstiltskin.

The thing that Daniel's rightly keying into is Oliver's complete trust and faith in the world around him. He's the friendliest furball we've ever met. And if someone were trying to attack me—or steal him—he'd lick that person's face. He'd drive the getaway car if he thought he could get string cheese out of it.

But what Oliver—if that is his real name—lacks in normal canine qualities, like loyalty, obedience and housetraining, he more than makes up for in adorableness and fearlessness.

It's not just that he isn't afraid of strangers. He isn't afraid of anything.

The only experience that's ever given him pause was his first exposure to a noisy vacuum cleaner, but even that he got over quickly. He hid under the coffee table for a few minutes before snorting, as if to announce he would be making a grand entrance. He then emerged from the table, walked slowly over to the appliance and started humping it. I'm told the humping isn't sexual at this age; it's about dominance and play. I admire the way he's literally trying to conquer his fears.

I often wish I were more like Oliver, that I could just chase down my fears and try to have sex with them. Instead, I'm cautious and fearful, analytical when I should carefree. Instead of living life and enjoying it, I scan the room to make sure everything is OK.

I've always been this way. I can remember staying after school with my teacher and my mom in second grade. Together, the two women were going to try to help me over my fear of the jungle gym by giving me all the time I needed—away from my peers —to climb and hang and swing and perhaps even do a flip off the bars one day, just like the other kids.

I showed those two dreamers by slipping and knocking out a tooth. Granted, it was a baby tooth, and they're meant to come out. But there was a lot of blood and a lot of sand. Is there anything more disgusting and more reminiscent of childhood than a mouthful of hot, bloody sand?

I've always lacked coordination, which is why I'm afraid of things that require it. Or maybe it's the other way around: I'm uncoordinated because I'm afraid. But the point is I'm afraid of things I'm not good at, and I'm not afraid of things I am good at. Public speaking? No problem. Parasailing? I'd rather stay here on firm, dry land.

My parents are similarly fearful. And despite their best intentions to impart an adventurous, lionhearted warrior spirit on their daughters, they instead passed along hay fever, cautiousness and birthing hips.

For this reason, I've decided to have Oliver raise my children.

Don't tell Daniel.

ooo

How I Feel About Your Bathroom Scale

Whenever I walk into someone's guest bathroom for the first time and see a scale sitting out—in case guests should want to weigh themselves during a dinner party, one assumes—I reflect on the way I would never ever casually step on another woman's scale, certainly not without the proper emotional preparation, and definitely not after any sort of salty hors d'oeuvres.

Then, while slowly backing away from the scale and making a cross with my fingers, I become envious of the casual and easy relationship with weight I imagine other people must have.

"Let's just have a look-see," I picture them saying before hopping onto the scale—probably with their shoes on.

These kinds of people only ever gain or lose half a pound. They could weigh themselves immediately following

Thanksgiving dinner—with a Tupperware full of leftovers in one hand and a cinderblock in the other—and their weight would be the same, give or take half a pound.

I merely look at yams and gain 10 pounds. This is why my relationship with the scale is much more complicated.

At any given time, my scale, which I've had for about 10 years, is in one of three places. It's in its usual spot in the bathroom, where I will be tempted to step on it at regular intervals like a nervous homeowner repeatedly checking the locks; on its side behind some towels (when I fear the number will be discouraging and I don't want to debate weighing myself every time I see it); or under the bed in another room (when it's been bad and needs a timeout).

And when I do step on it, I don't do so lightly, no pun intended. I rip off every possible article of clothing and jewelry— if I could temporarily donate a kidney I would—and then mount the scale with the solemnity of someone entering a confessional. I close my eyes, hold my breath, say a quick prayer and then look down.

If I sound neurotic, which I do and which I am, it's because my weight has been up and down (usually more up than down) for many years of my life. Though I've managed to maintain a decent weight loss for a while now, I'm convinced those 40 pounds are waiting for the chance—plotting, really—to snap back onto my body. To this end, I torture myself by thinking at all times about what I'm putting in my mouth, what I'm going to be putting in my mouth or what I already put in my mouth.

I recently had one of those weeks where I thought it best to avoid the scale, as I knew it would only lead to a bad mood. Instead, I told myself, I would diet and exercise and then weigh myself in a few days. But as always happens, at a certain point, I became convinced that by giving myself a break from the internal hectoring I was allowing those pounds to creep back on. And so, I just had to get on the scale and live in reality, even if it's a reality in which I'd gained 20 pounds in three days.

I gave myself an insane pep talk and hopped on to discover I'd lost a pound.

This was impossible.

Instead of feeling relief, I was convinced the scale was broken and that it had probably been broken for years. Who knows how long this generous scale had been blowing smoke up my butt?

I set off to find things around the house that I could weigh to test its accuracy. I started with two cartoons of milk. The scale didn't register them at all, which had me convinced it's at least two milk cartons short. I tried to weigh my 6-pound puppy, but he was too squirmy. Then I remembered my fiancé has some dumbbells. I placed two 10-pound weights on the scale. Nineteen pounds. I did this repeatedly, relieved the scale was only 1 pound off.

But any comfort I experienced soon gave way to panic when it occurred to me that perhaps the scale was off 1 pound for every 20 pounds. How would I know? I discussed the matter with my fiancé, who suggested that I just put another 20 pounds on the scale.

The good news is the scale wasn't broken. The bad news is it is now because one of the weights slipped out of my hand and crashed onto it, cracking the readout.

Or maybe that's the good news?

ooo

On Being a Woman in Comedy and Podcasting

I'm often asked what it's like to be a woman in the male-dominated fields of comedy and podcasting. This question—like "What is your favorite movie?" or "Why didn't you call me back?"—isn't very fun to answer, which is why I usually don't.

I'll say: "Hmm. That's a good question," as if an opportunity to ruminate and expound were a gift seldom bestowed upon me. Then I'll pause thoughtfully for a moment, point to something that isn't there, shriek and slide under the table until the subject changes.

I realize I'm part of the problem with my disingenuous answer. Here's a tip: If you ask a question that's greeted with "good question," it's not a good question. I know this seems counterintuitive, and I, too, have fallen for it. "Look at me asking the tough questions like a regular Barbara Walters or Kermit the Frog 'Newsflash,'" I've crowed to myself upon having my question complimented. In fact, so enamored was I of my own inquisitiveness that I didn't even notice whether the question was being answered.

But back to the one I'm currently not answering. I can only dodge it so many times, and lately it's been coming up with such frequency that I've finally decided to address it.

With the exception of the times a baby has unexpectedly shot out of my vagina and/or I've had to leave the stage to check on a soufflé, I'd say that my experience isn't all that different from a man's. Yes, I receive only 77 percent of each laugh. And sure, I've been told that with a tan and a nose job I'd be "good to go." But that's just because I'm unfunny and pale, and I have a nose the size of Montenegro. I don't see it when I look in the mirror, but someone said so on YouTube, so it must be true.

Now, I know what you're thinking: Montenegro isn't even that big. And you're right. For a country, it's very small. But for a nose, it's big.

As for the issue of whether there are more funny men or more funny women, I literally can't answer, what with not being good at math and always having bonbons in my mouth.

In terms of material, women are free to do many of the same subjects as men so long as they never talk about their personal lives, struggles to find a mate, weight, menstruation, insecurities or, if they have them, children. These topics are considered too "hacky," and the last thing you want to be is hacky—unless you're ugly, in which case ugly is the last thing you want to be. In order of things you don't want to be: fat, hacky, ugly, smelly, angry.

Instead, why not pick a few traits from the following list: nice, floral, breakfasty, thoughtful, booby, cute, gluten-free, petite, maternal, perky, Kate Upton-like, serene or hairless (exception: hair on the head)? Who wouldn't laugh at a hairless, gluten-free, booby comedian doing jokes about something completely gender neutral that affects us all, like itchy balls?

As for my process, I imagine it's no different than a guy's, except for that one week a month when I retire to a special Wi-Fi-enabled hut, where I attempt to be funny in between crying jags. During this time, I also light scented candles, scrapbook and yell at everyone.

So those are my silly little thoughts on what it's like to be a woman working in a male-dominated field. But if you really want to know, you should probably ask a man because all this thinking has tired me out.

The question I think people are really getting at when they ask me about my experience is, why aren't there more women in these fields? There are a lot, to be sure. Probably more now than ever. But the perception is that comedy and podcasting are still heavily male, and I do have some thoughts about that.

While I believe both sexes are equally capable of humor, it's historically been less socially acceptable for a woman to be funny because humor, even the most benign, self-deprecating humor, still has a scintilla of aggression, and women are encouraged to be gentle and agreeable. A woman who's funny, who shows that kind of messy, electrifying, sometimes combative engagement with the world, will be given a bit of a wider berth.

Now, if you'll excuse me, I'm going to crawl under the table.

ooo

It's Getting Hot, so I'm Moving to Antarctica

It's now that time of year when it goes from slightly warm to holy-hell-I-think-I'm-sitting-on-the-face-of-the-sun overnight, which is excellent news for the 1 percent of us who enjoy their upper arms and a natural disaster for the rest of us.

Listen, you Gwyneths in your sleeveless tunics and your spaghetti strap sundresses and, worst of all, your blouses with cap sleeves that make my white noodles look like the beginning of a balloon animal. All of you can go confidently hail a cab into the ocean. My former co-worker who looked forward to summer because she was "allergic to sleeves" can be your driver.

You're ruining it for the rest of us with your cocoa-buttered, bronzed, sculpted limbs that are the same size whether they're pressed against your body or you're not so self-consciously reaching for something on a high shelf.

You're the kind of nightmares who could probably be wearing a short T-shirt, reach up to smoothe your perfect hair and then put your arm down without worrying you just exposed a shocking white ripple of albino muffin top. You disgust me. I can barely go from seated to standing without having to readjust everything.

The appropriate reaction to mercury rising is dread and anxiety. The weather is not your friend, or if it is, it's that friend who "accidentally" tells everyone your most unflattering secrets, which in this case are flabby arms, thighs that stick together and my upper lip's tendency to form beads of sweat. And frizz. Oh, and the fact that when I'm warm, my face flushes and turns red, especially my nose. Why couldn't we be trending toward global cooling? I could get behind that.

I very nearly wore a tank top to therapy yesterday because it was so hot that the part of my brain that regulates shirts was scrambled, and I figured if I'm going to do it, it should at least be in a room in which the person gets paid at the end. But at the last minute, I couldn't force the sight of my white, wobbly, freckle-and-mole covered monstrosities on to another person, not even one I tell my darkest secrets to.

But there's one more secret she doesn't know: My upper arms also have a light dusting of ... What do you think I'm going to say here? Let's play a guessing game. Is it powdered sugar? Glitter? Rainbows? Happy faces? Raised pink dots irritated to varying degrees (and maybe a little dried blood) because I like to pick at them when I'm bored because sometimes you can find and liberate an ingrown hair? Ding, ding, ding!

I've read a million articles in women's magazines that purport to get your arms ready for summer in five easy steps. Which summer are we talking about? Nuclear summer? Camus' invincible summer? Summer 2040? Or the one a few weeks away? If it's that one, I just don't think a few arm curls are going to do it. I need something faster. Can't they just paint on some muscles and shade the rest? Where are we with arm-painting technology? You don't hear enough about trompe l'arm.

And I hate that I'm wasting this much time thinking about my arms when I have so many more important things to think about, like my hair.

The other day, I went clothes shopping with my mother because I was in a good mood and wanted it to dissipate.

"So, let me ask you this," I said, turning to her in a tank top, my upper arms undulating like a just-vacated waterbed. "If I were to wear this in public, would the reaction be like, 'There goes a fat person?' Or 'There goes a small person with fat arms?'"

She looked at me like she questioned whether I'd really been going to therapy.

I think I've been convinced this whole time—after weight loss and exercise and dieting and growing up—that there's still something about my body, or something about me, really, that, if it were exposed would change the entire way I come across, and possibly even jeopardize relationships and employment. And all the exhausting work I've done to be the person I am today would simply disappear, and I'd be standing there, awkward, fat, frizzy and scared, all because I exposed a flabby arm. Or thigh. Or sweat 'stache. The thing is, the body part I'm convinced I have to hide—the physical portal to the past—keeps changing. That's probably because it's a feeling more than anything.

It's for this reason I have no choice but to move to Antarctica. I realize I can't outrun my arms or my past. But I'd rather face them in a jacket.

ooo

The Impossible Shower

My favorite sensation is that of having just taken a shower, when I'm feeling clean, smooth, refreshed and like I've accomplished something—namely, showering. My second favorite sensation is that of being in the shower under the nozzle, enveloped by steam and hot water. My third is being left alone with a breadbasket and an overflowing leprechaun pot's worth of gold foil-covered packets of butter, but that's beside the point.

Considering my feelings about showering, you might imagine I spring from the sheets in the morning and make a beeline for the shower, a smile on my face and a song in my heart, ready to face another great day. You might imagine this, but you'd be sorely mistaken. What kind of asshole do you think I am?

On the contrary, I waste inordinate amounts of time trying to find the motivation to shower. It's as if an impenetrable force field surrounds the bathroom and I'm trapped on the outside with Google and Twitter and a million distractions. I love feeling clean, but apparently, what I love more is Googling episodes of TV shows I saw when I was so young that I'm left wondering whether I imagined them. In the case of the episode of "Facts of Life" that was a send-up of "The Twilight Zone," where Blair was moussed to death, it really existed.

If someone told me how much time I would spend as an adult trying to figure out how to manage my time, I never would have believed them. I'd say a good third of my day is spent figuring out when to shower. Another third is spent trying to figure out how to shave my armpits in a way that both removes hair and doesn't leave me looking and feeling as if I slid pits first on a bumpy gravel road. The last third is spent debating insignificant online purchases. It's amazing I get anything done.

But every time I mention the shower issue, people tell me how they relate. If you aren't relating, it's likely you work normal daytime hours. Consider yourself among the lucky—and very mature.

For those of us who work evenings, as I do, or work freelance or work from home or are unemployed, structuring a day can prove challenging, especially if you have nowhere to go and no one to see. Why waste all that grooming?

I remember when the conservation of grooming began. It was when I was in my late teens and early 20s, when the idea of staying home on a Friday night was unthinkable but most plans were made at the last minute. Because it took me forever to get ready, I would begin the process early in the day, on the off chance I'd have somewhere to go.

These were the days before Brazilian or Japanese hair straightening, when if you had curly hair and wanted to wear it straight, which I always did, you had to rely on a blow dryer, a paddle brush, some kind of oily pomade and a drought. The longer you ran the blow dryer, the hotter you would get, and the sweat and heat coming off your head would make the sections of hair you'd already straightened curl again. You would focus your attention on one location, and frizz would spring up in another. It was like whack-a-mole but on my scalp. All of this was to achieve a damaged swirl of dry frizzy hair that in no way resembled the naturally straight flowing locks I coveted.

Imagine taking a cotton ball and stretching it out until it was kind of flat and rectangular. And then imagine it being black and giant and protruding from the back of my head. That's what my hair looked like. And it took me hours to achieve that look.

Then there was the makeup and the accessories and the trying and retrying of all the clothes in my closet, all of which was done on spec. I basically set aside the entire day to appear spontaneous. If I ended up not going out, I felt awful and foolish because I'd spent so much time getting ready. And for what? To sit by the phone? It was a waste of mascara.

So maybe that's why the pendulum has swung so far in the other direction. I basically won't start getting ready until it's too late for me to be on time.

I should Google time management.

ooo

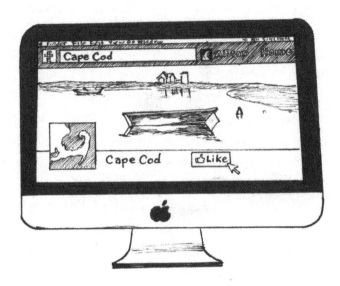

My Imaginary Cape Friends

The person I wish I was is far more social than the person it seems I am. I say "it seems" because I still hold out hope that one day I'll wake up a completely different person—one who prefers capri pants to sweats and summers at a beachfront cottage on some sort of cape with several other witty and charming couples.

Nights at this balmy locale would be spent drinking wine and playing bunco or bridge, neither of which I know how to play. Days would involve gaiety of some sort on or near a pier, and perhaps a sumptuous stroll into town. Everything would be breezy and glamorous and fun, save for that lively disagreement—the kind we'd reference for years after—over how to prepare fresh lobster.

Perhaps it would turn into an annual vacation and I'd have a whole wardrobe of sarongs and hats. I'd probably keep them in a steamer trunk with a label that says, "For the Cape," along with other precious keepsakes.

In this alternate universe—inspired by a J.Crew catalog—I'm living a fabulous life made rich and meaningful through dazzling get-togethers, galas, social outings, tennis matches, heart-to-hearts, laughter and great friendship, like something in between "The Great Gatsby" and "The Sisterhood of the Traveling Pants."

In real life, I mostly hang out alone or with my fiancé and stay loosely connected to all my friends via Facebook, Twitter and email. Some days, I decide that I really *must* make the time to get together with this person or that person, as they are old friends, the kind you can just pick up with after time has passed and it feels exactly the same. Then I'll blink and two years will have gone by, and I'll realize I haven't done it. And that's fine, sort of, except I'm afraid this is how it could go for the rest of my life: putting off seeing friends in two-year increments until one day I die. It's depressing.

So then I say to myself, "I should just have a party and invite all the friends I haven't seen in forever and catch up with all of them at once." I do long to be the party-hosting kind. But when was the last time you had a meaningful conversation with anyone at a party? Somehow, you end up saying hi and bye to the people you want to talk to and spending the rest of the time buttonholed by Sheila's cousin who just left a big agency to open a boutique PR firm, and can she connect with you on LinkedIn?

It's gotten to the point where as I'm putting on my bra to leave the house—an act I regard as a gift I give to the world and a sign that I'm playing by *their* rules, since if left to my own devices, I'd shuffle around in an oversized T-shirt and sweatpants—I soothe my mounting anxiety by telling myself that in a few short, sweet hours I will be able to return home to my comfortable state of braless torpor.

There are extroverts; there are introverts; and then there's me, someone who is folding in on herself. That's how much I don't feel like leaving the house to make small talk.

Granted, I have my moments, as well as a career that involves stretches of extreme extroverted activity. But the vast majority of the time I feel like my batteries are drained and I need a nap. And so help me, if the phone rings, I'm sending it to voicemail faster than you can say, "I actually enjoy talking to that person, but now is a bad time."

In this alternate universe, though, when the phone rings I jump on it because it could be Sue or Karen or Millie or any of my many, many friends from the cape. I don't hear from my cape friends very often because we're all living such dynamic and fulfilling and busy lives. But when I do, I seize upon the opportunity to catch up. Hours pass in a reverie of laughter and memories and sometimes even tears of joy. Of course, there goes the afternoon! It looks like someone won't be playing croquet, but that's just what happens when you're reminiscing about clambakes with Karen.

Incidentally, her full name is TedandKaren. All my cape friends are one half of a dynamic couple. There's DougAndSue, TedandKaren and BiffandMillie. There's also ArtandArlene, but they're dead to me ever since Arlene ripped the last haddock right from my hands at the local fishmonger. I mean, have you ever? I have never.

In *this* universe, though, I not only don't hang out with these couples. I don't even know anyone with these names. I've got a real shortage of one-and-two syllable '70s names and a surplus of Mikes. If anyone needs a Mike, I'll trade you for a Karen, Ted or Sue.

I want to say the reason I'm not living this extended montage of a life—like the one I think my parents lived at my age—is that today we get our fill of fellow human beings at our jobs. The way we live and work now—putting career before just about everything, being connected to our jobs around the clock (by that I mean always looking at Twitter)—leaves very little left for clambakes and the like. I want it to be that and not my own shortcoming.

Now, if you'll excuse me, Millie's cousin Tilly is in town, and my presence is requested on the pier.

ooo

The Highway Is Trying to Kill Me

Yesterday, on our way up the coast to look at wedding venues, my fiancé and I found ourselves on the business end of a wee fender benderoony, which is my cute name for something unpleasant that will likely be a costly and aggravating time suck.

It wasn't our fault, mind you. But from what everyone tells me, fault and blame are neither here nor there when it comes to car accidents.

While my fiancé handled the details, I sat dazed in the passenger seat thinking about how much car accident protocol has changed.

In my day, shortly after I got my license, when I was nowhere near ready to drive despite what the state of California thought, an accident involved pulling over and then nervously sitting in your car, hoping the person who emerged from the dented vehicle in front of you didn't want to kill you.

To this end, you screwed up your face into an approximation of tears and said sorry a zillion times, even though your insurance company would later tell you that was a mistake.

If this worked to neutralize the anger coming at you, you shuffled around your overstuffed glove compartment, sifting through batteries, perfume, a tangle of sunglasses, an unopened compass (this was way before GPS) that seemed like a good purchase at the time, a flashlight, lip gloss and cassettes (both of which were melting) and fished out your registration.

Then you exchanged information and tried to scribble down the other person's details, even though your hand was shaking uncontrollably.

After this, you found the nearest pay phone to call your parents.

Now, everyone just calmly snaps photos on their iPhone.

"You OK?" asked one of the drivers, tapping on my window. She'd been in a car that had both gotten hit and hit someone else.

I nodded.

Once we were back on the road, my fiancé, who held it together during the photo-snapping but whose hand was now curling into a ball—an upsetting new trick he didn't know was in his body's repertoire—reminded me that we'd very nearly gotten into an accident a year before on this same stretch of highway.

And then, proving that immunity is a thing that only exists on reality shows, a car almost swerved into us in roughly the same spot on the way back.

I'm not a superstitious person, but what the hell?

If this is a sign, and that's a big if, what is it a sign of?

That we should avoid this road?

That we shouldn't get married north of Los Angeles County?

That we shouldn't get married at all?

Again, I'm not a superstitious person, save for a refusal to wake up when the clock is on a zero or a five (Everyone wakes up on a zero or a five. I prefer 8:01 a.m.!) and a marked incredulity when people tempt fate by opening umbrellas indoors. But I was beginning to wonder whether we're taking our life in our hands.

It sounds preposterous, but 100 percent of the time we've driven to Santa Barbara we've either had to swerve to avoid an accident or gotten in one.

What is the meaning of this?

I want to say it means nothing because that makes me the most comfortable and is most in accordance with my (lack of) belief system. But the truth is, I'm afraid to make the drive again.

I'm reminded of my dating days, when there was a disparity between my head and my heart.

I frequently found myself in the situation where I liked someone and wanted it to work out but felt some combination of negative emotions every time I saw the person.

So much of growing up has been about learning to trust my feelings even when my intellect is trying to reason them away, which is all good and fine, except when you know the feelings— like the ones I'm having now regarding a particular stretch of the 101 freeway—are irrational.

I am an atheist. I believe in nothing. And yet I'm honestly entertaining the notion that the universe may be trying to tell me something and/or out to get me.

And the real kick in the heinie is that we kind of fell in love with the first venue we saw, the one in Santa Barbara on the other side of the highway that's trying to kill us.

I ask you, what would you do?

And don't say "arrive by helicopter or horse" because I've seen "The Bachelorette" and I'm pretty sure that's bad luck.

ooo

Blame the Car

I've never really thought of myself as a car person, let alone a car snob. My favorite car is the one someone else is driving, and if I ever win the lottery, I'm going to hire a chauffer so I can sit in an air-conditioned vehicle alternately snoozing and checking Twitter. I'm also going to install a salad bar in my living room, but that's neither here nor there.

I'm currently in the market for a new car, so I've been dragging anyone willing (and some who aren't) with me on test drives. I was recently explaining my car philosophy to someone, that I'm a level-headed person who just needs a safe, reliable functioning car, nothing fancy, when my younger sister began clearing her throat.

Apparently, she's still upset about a certain very baffling weekend during which I discovered behind the right set of wheels that I go from zero to maniac in a matter of minutes.

We were living in New York City at the time, and I was working for a magazine that was putting together a travel issue.

The theme was road trips. We were each supposed to set out on a jaunt in a different car and then record our impressions. I didn't specifically ask for a fully loaded convertible sports car, but I didn't turn it down either. How was I supposed to know it would change me?

I'm normally a cautious driver, but suddenly I was doing 90 mph, darting in and out of traffic, honking impatiently at blue hairs and, most troublingly, smiling smugly at my fellow sports car-driving motorists.

"Can we please put the top up?" pleaded my increasingly frizzy-haired sister as we zipped down the highway on our way to Stonington, Connecticut, about 140 miles away. I may have pretended I didn't hear her, as I wasn't about to let her requests or the fact that it was beginning to rain interfere with my full enjoyment of the convertible.

We'd cobbled together a tour of coastal southern Connecticut, but at the last minute I decided that instead of staying at a cheesy but fun-looking hotel, we should stay at a luxurious inn.

The person who drives this car belongs at an inn.

I am the person who is driving this car.

I belong at an inn.

But it was the wrong call; the 18-room bed and breakfast was lovely but not for us, seeing as we neither owned yachts nor had sex with each other.

After dinner, we strolled back through the sleepy town to our romantic private room with a fireplace and a single king bed.

"Just stay on your side," my sister hissed before slamming off the light.

And that's when it started: the need to get back in the car. My fingers yearned to grip the steering wheel. My feet ached to grace the pedals. In the space of a day, I'd formed a relationship with the car that verged on sexual. I couldn't get it out of my mind!

The next day, we ventured into Mystic and strolled along the cute seaside shops, peeked our heads into Mystic Pizza—like the movie—and then hit the aquarium. (Side note: Why must all aquariums smell like sardines and seal piss? Is there not some kind of industrial-strength Febreze that could tackle this odor? Or a giant scented candle? I went through a candle phase in college, and all my belongings from that time still reek. I have textbooks that smell like honeydew. Let's get on this, people.)

Then, in an effort to bring my miserable sister around, I suggested The Mohegan Sun casino and resort, situated on land owned by the Mohegan tribe, which was really only about 20 minutes from Mystic, give or take the five hours I tacked on for scenic motoring.

I would have happily driven to Canada; that's how close I was to achieving the Platonic ideal of fahrvergnugen. But my wind-whipped sister, by this point looking like the Unabomber with only a tiny sliver of face showing behind sunglasses and a hoodie pulled tightly around her head, didn't share my devil-may-care attitude.

Once at the casino, where we were shown to our room by a woman named "Walks Alone," whom I heard refer to herself as Paula on the phone, we settled in for a rejuvenating couple days of swimming and relaxing.

I would have rather been driving the whole time.

"Do you want to dri-?" Do you want to dri-?" I kept trying to ask my sister. I was thinking that perhaps if she got a taste of Carlos—oh, yes, did I mention I gave the car a name?—she might feel less like she'd been hoodwinked into coming on a three-day test drive disguised as a fun trip. But I couldn't get the word all the way out. It was stuck!

As a concession, I agreed to keep the top up on the drive home. And I only went a few hours out of our way.

ooo

Tropical Attire Encouraged

A friend of mine has been texting me nonstop today to find out whether I'm going to a Tiki party tonight. Clearly he doesn't know me well. If there's one thing I don't like, it's a good time. And if there's another, it's a costume party that demands skimpy attire, which is the only kind of costume party there is.

Can't we have some kind of "warm your tootsies by the fire" snow party where you're encouraged to come dressed as your favorite avalanche survivor?

Who are these people longing for a chance to take it all off? It's currently summer in Los Angeles. How many more pieces can be removed before we're just naked?

I realize I sound like an awful prude, and that isn't it at all. I'm very liberated in spirit. I'm just not liberated in wardrobe. I'm all for being as free as you want. I just don't want to have to join in because I have a mind made for fast living and a body made for Norway. Is it cold in Norway? You get what I'm saying.

Have you ever seen one of those eggs with a shell that didn't form and harden all the way for some reason, so it's kind of pinkish and soft and translucent? You might need to have spent significant time with an egg-laying chicken or duck, which I have (long story), to know what I'm talking about. But anyway, that's the color of my skin: deformed eggshell.

I'm also wobbly and squishy. I have abs in there, but I don't know how many. If a great set of abs is a six-pack, then I think I might have a four-pack of something soft, like Capri Sun. You could try to bounce a quarter off my juice-pouch abs, but it would hurt, so please don't.

But back to this soiree and the texts I'm ignoring: The invite says "tropical attire encouraged." I like that it's not so pushy as to say "dress code enforced," which is up there with "no substitutions" in terms of rules that make me want to break them just because *you're not the boss of me.* But I also find it a bit misleading because I guarantee if I show up in my preferred summerwear of jeans and a sweater, I will be the only one.

And then I will have to field the question "Aren't you hot?" all night.

Do you know how hard it is to shake your head and say you're actually quite comfortable while wiping beads of sweat off your upper lip and fanning yourself with a dirty paper plate? Here's a trick: As you go through the buffet line, "accidentally" grab two paper plates. Then you won't be spraying yourself with macaroni salad, which, while refreshing, is murder on a black sweater.

And here's another tip for people like me who prefer the security of outerwear. If it happens to be cold out but you continue to wear a jacket indoors because this is how you feel most comfortable and attractive, people will constantly ask whether you're cold. You will want to say yes as an explanation for why you're wearing the coat. "I tend to run cold," you will be tempted to say, hoping the way you're holding a frosty root beer against your forehead while perched next to the fan and panting isn't giving you away. Take it from me: Don't do it! If you do, then your gracious host will turn up the heat and, in essence, cook you right out of your jacket.

One of the scariest nights of my life involved a date I was on where the guy kept cranking the heat because I was saying I was cold. When I finally couldn't take it anymore and went to take off the jacket, he balked. "No, leave it on," he murmured into my sweaty ear. "Let's pretend we're at a ski resort!" I'm not sure if he was trying to seduce me or kill me, but it was far too hot for any kind of role play.

"How about I'll be a skier and you be a snowboarder, and I'll do my best to avoid you?" I suggested as I stuck my head in the freezer.

So anyway, I probably won't be going to the party, but I will be turning up the AC and having my own Winter Wonderland party of one. Well, one and a half if you count my dog that's always wearing fur. Sweaters encouraged.

ooo

Please Stop Yelling in a Little Box

I really don't know how to feel about all this NSA stuff. It's complicated and nuanced, and I find myself going back and forth. Am I the only one? I can't imagine I am, and yet every time I turn on the TV there's someone in a little box yelling in a way that suggests he or she knows exactly how I'm supposed to feel.

And by "little box" I'm not referring to the TV itself. TVs are no longer little boxes. They are giant rectangles mounted in all manner of places, increasingly including the outdoors. Because what's a barbecue without a giant orange legal analyst yelling at you about the government?

No, by "little boxes" I'm referring to all the talking heads beamed onto the screen at once who are yelling at one another and you, often all at the same time, like a monstrous "Brady Bunch" fever dream.

There was a time when having a nuanced, measured, well-considered take on something, one that didn't fit neatly into, well, a box, was appreciated. Those days are gone.

Today you have to turn your opinion into a slogan and make it as loud and attention-grabbing as possible.

Despite what cynics say, it's not that the news only wants to present one side. It's that it wants to present one side per person. Instead of having a single voice canvass the issue, which feels calm and mature, the preference is to have two or more people—best if they hate each other—go head-to-head with the goal of never agreeing, like a blood sport.

And it's a real shame because this process takes once-intelligent viewpoints and exaggerates them to the point where they're no longer recognizable, pumping them full of hot air and stripping them of subtlety. If opinions were people, these ones walked in looking like folks you went to high school with and walked out looking like the women on the "Real Housewives of Orange County"—giant lips, big boobs and kind of entertaining to watch, but what the hell was that?

I don't understand why we've abandoned the idea of complexity. It's the one best-suited for the world we live in. Complexity exists in pockets—newspaper articles that are TL;DR (an online acronym for "too long; didn't read"); dry NPR broadcasts; people who speak in a British accent. But you really have to seek these out. By contrast, opinions that are simplified and yelled are everywhere. The media has turned into a live breathing all-caps 24-hour Twitter feed.

And I'm not just talking about what I witness as a spectator. I've been on the inside of the opinion factory, and I've seen how the opinions are made. It happens like this: A producer of a news show contacts you and says the host wants to do a segment about

a certain issue and needs someone to argue a certain side. Is that
you? And then, if you say yes, you will be expected to be frothing
at the mouth to argue this one side. Should you allow nuance into
your argument, you will feel you've let them down just a little.
They wanted a cockfight. You gave them rhythmic gymnastics.

And the thing is, everyone involved will actually understand
what happened because they know they've simplified something
complex into opposing bits of pabulum. They themselves
probably fall somewhere in the middle, as any sentient being
would. But you see, they didn't bring you on to be sentient, or to
be a human being. They brought you on to sit in a box and yell.

It's a shame because it's not as if we, the public, demand this
oversimplification. The popularity of shows like "Mad Men,"
"Game of Thrones" and "The Sopranos" proves we're very good at
hanging out in the uncertain middle ground, exploring the space
between the extremes, calibrating our sympathies and affection
for people and worlds that are very clearly both good and bad. In
fact, we enjoy puzzling through contradictions.

But back to the NSA stuff. I find I'm just not as appalled as I
get the feeling I should be. Is it because the ramifications are so
abstract? Or because I suspected this was going on anyway? Or
because I have nothing to hide?

And yet, it's not as if I'm totally fine with it either, because I
don't think we really know yet the full scope of the surveillance
and in what way it's been wielded.

I have to assume there are more of me—people who are
somewhere in the middle—than there are of them—people whose
extreme certainty knows no bounds.

We just aren't yelling about it.

ooo

The Uninvited Houseguest

I lived in New York for almost 10 years and was lucky enough to never see a cockroach in my apartment. I saw plenty of other unpleasant things—mice, a junkie throwing up in my kitchen sink, an air conditioning unit in the process of falling from its perch in the window (I shrieked and pulled it in by the extension cord) and my hair after a hard rain—but never a cockroach.

Now I live in Los Angeles, where I've traded in gritty realness for a better, cheaper apartment with wall-to-wall carpeting, modern amenities and a parking space. All the downsides of urban living are supposed to be behind me, so I was somewhat alarmed to peer over at the bathroom counter (Oh, and I have counters. Bite me, pedestal sinks!) to find a cockroach the size of a small egg roll hanging out near my soap dish.

Instead of the kind of insect I usually find—some kind of wispy-winged creature that's long and thready and disintegrates into nearly nothing when you smush it—a roach has substance. It's crunchy and jarring.

In a flash, I wondered how long he'd been there and whether he'd taken any detours through my makeup brushes and face soap, which were sitting out uncovered. And why was he so close to my retainer case? Granted, I haven't worn my retainers in years, but that could change any day so long as it doesn't mean risking roach detritus.

He seemed kind of still, so I grabbed an empty container of false eyelashes, which is a flimsy plastic box, and attempted to trap my uninvited guest. Unfortunately, he resisted re-homing and scurried into the sink.

I shrieked. It was time to call in reinforcements.

"Large bug! Large bug!" I yelled to my fiancé.

He got a look, gasped and threw his shoe in the sink.

"Did I get it?" he yelled from across the room.

"No!" I responded, standing on the toilet.

He removed his other shoe and made another hole in one, which didn't graze the bug either.

I questioned this strategy. What if he had angered the roach?

Then, acting on pure impulse, he fished a shoe from the sink and whacked the bug. The fact that he's still wearing these shoes is freaking me out.

For the rest of the day, I couldn't shake the feeling that things were amiss, a feeling that was perhaps exacerbated by helpful friends promising that if you have one roach, you probably have thousands.

As when we had mice in our apartment, I find myself wondering why I'm so disturbed. What is the genesis of the fear? In truth, I'm a lot bigger than these things. And mice can be cute—in a Disney film or even at a pet store. So why the panic?

People will say it's because these critters carry diseases and we've evolved to fear them, but I don't think it's that. I think it's the fear of little things crawling around or on your body, or up your leg and into your mouth.

At one point in New York, when I was most desperate and irrational but not yet ready to call in an exterminator (clearly what I should have done from the beginning), I tried to give the mice names. Perhaps if I were to view them as friendly creatures that happen to share my living space, I thought, I would be less upset by their presence.

It didn't work.

Plus, they never came when called.

Not willing to cede my domicile just yet, I turned to my dad for a solution. He's old; he doesn't like bugs. Maybe he would have some advice. Instead, he did that super annoying thing that old people do: got philosophical.

"Roaches and humans have been coexisting for millions and millions of years," he said. "They were probably living in caves with early man."

"Great," I said. "I don't want them in my bathroom."

Then the Confucius of entomology offered a comforting pearl of wisdom. He said: "They're all over. They're everywhere."

I resisted the urge to throw my shoe at him.

I told my landlord, and he brought an exterminator around. Have you ever noticed how exterminators are always sweaty? It's high-intensity work, this bug killing. Anyway, he asked me how big was the roach was. I told him. He determined this to mean that it had come in from the outside. I shudder to think about whether that means bigger or smaller ones are living inside.

He said he sprayed outside, so we really shouldn't have any more, but if we find another one, he'll come back and spray the lower cabinets.

I feel good that we have a plan, but I think we should move in the meantime.

ooo

Let's Get a Dog's Opinion

I realize everyone who knows anything about dogs says the humane thing to do is to spay or neuter them. My feeling has always been that it's really easy for us to say that, but let's get a dog's opinion. Somehow I suspect it would take a less hard-line stance.

Despite my misgivings, we just had our little guy neutered—because if you live in Los Angeles and don't neuter your pet, you will be run out of town by a screaming mob of people with pitchforks who shop at Whole Foods and do CrossFit. It was awful. For me, that is. Oliver seemed fine.

But back to me. The vet told us to drop Oliver off in the morning between 7:30 a.m. and 9 a.m. My fiancé and I arrived a little before 9 a.m. and waited about an hour before anyone took us in. This afforded us ample time to feel guilty (me), nap (Oliver), question what we were doing (me), read news stories on our iPhone (Daniel), look around nervously (me), watch a video about cat parasites (all of us) and whine (Oliver and me).

I get that we live in a very crowded world, but I remember a time when the term "waiting room" wasn't so literal and seeing a doctor didn't involve sitting in the aforementioned room for at least an hour. These days, going to the gynecologist for an annual checkup is an all-day affair.

And don't even get me started on how you wait in the waiting room for an hour, and then the nurse finally takes you into the exam room and weighs you, takes your blood pressure, asks a bunch of nosy questions and says, "The doctor will be in shortly," only for you to wait for another eternity.

At the very least, how about the medical community provide us with something more entertaining to pass the time than a plastic model of our reproductive organs, a video about "ablation" (I don't know what it is, and I don't want to know) and a bunch of parenting magazines? How about personal satellite TVs and a quesadilla station?

But back to the vet. While we were waiting—and I was repeatedly apologizing to Daniel because I expected this to be a quick thing but now he was late for work—I kept looking around at all the pets that were nowhere near as cute as Oliver. I mean, it was truly one ugly dog after the other.

By the time we were finally called, I was experiencing full-on paranoia, wondering whether the people who work there really love animals as much as they pretend they do. What if the minute we leave they turn into Disney villains? What if this is the last time I'll see Oliver because something horrible will happen to him on the tiny operating table, all because I signed him up for a procedure I was second-guessing?

It was more than I could bear. I drowned my sorrows in stale cookies from a jar with a sign reading, "These treats are for humans." If I had to stay there any longer, I would have sampled the complimentary dog and cat treats as well because fear makes me hungry.

I went home and waited and waited and waited and waited. And then, I waited some more. "I should really take advantage of this time to do all the things I can't do when Oliver is here," I thought to myself. I kicked off my shoes and socks and left them right in the middle of the floor. I opened all the doors, ate string cheese without being sneaky and watered some hanging plants without having to hold the pots over my head so as to avoid the tendrils dragging on the floor. It was a real party, but I couldn't shake the feeling that this is what it would be like if Oliver were gone.

When the nurse told me over the phone that everything went fine and I could come pick him up, I cried a little because I am ridiculous.

Recovery was fast, and I learned a couple of valuable lessons: Getting your dog neutered in Los Angeles costs more than getting your appendix removed in another town, and if I ever have children, I'm going to think twice before getting them fixed.

ooo

I'm Afraid of Fun

Now that July 4 is safely behind us, I must confess something that may change how you feel about me: I hate firecrackers. I don't just dislike them. I hate them. HATE them. Haaaaaaaaaaaate them.

I hate when teenagers light them in the street; I hate when friends fire them off balconies; and I particularly hate when someone decides to modify them. This kicks the whole experience up a notch from terrifying to panic-inducing soil-my-pants.

And why is it that everyone must collect in the street to watch the lighting of the modified firecrackers? Can't I enjoy the delicious exhilaration of wondering whether I'm going to lose any fingers or eyes from inside the house behind a comforting bowl of guacamole? Is it absolutely necessary that I join the masses? I'm just going to ruin everyone's fun with my "Is it supposed to do that?" and "Are you sure this is legal?" and "Oh, these? I always wear safety goggles."

Dogs really have an edge when it comes to disliking explosives. Everyone accepts that dogs freak out around both fireworks and firecrackers, so people keep them far away or put them in dog anxiety jackets, which are real things that I wish came in people size. The only thing us anxious humans can do is drink alcohol, which seems like a bad idea when the goal is to avoid being extra flammable.

And for the record, I also dislike barbecues, the beach, football and hot tubs.

I'm as un-American as apple clafouti.

Here's my question: Are there people who actually go nuts for barbecues? There must be. There must be people who love barbecues as much as I love my favorite activity: looking at pictures of ducklings on the internet.

I wish I were the kind of person who leapt from the sheets on July 4 excited to slap on a bunch of sunscreen and stand in the hot sun swatting at flies and flipping meat. Just the feel of grass poking through my sandal is enough to make me long for winter. Hell, just wearing sandals does it. The human foot wasn't meant to be partially caged in strappy leather. It was meant to be fully caged in some kind of oxford or boot.

But the thing is, I want people to think I'm fun. I want them to think I'm fun, spontaneous and always up for a good time. I want them to think I'm like one of those fun girls with beachy waves and a wraparound skirt sitting in the back of a Jeep in a beer commercial. Perhaps I play sand volleyball. Maybe I bring my golden retriever to the beach. I could possibly wave flirtatiously while snow skiing.

In my fantasies, I'm the kind of person who might yell "woo" atop some weenie's shoulders, start the wave, employ a sky writer or join a drum circle. Will I ride a Ski-Doo backward? Will I board a small unsafe-looking boat in choppy water? Will I make out with you on a Ferris wheel?

Yes, yes and YES!

I mean, in reality, no. Never. But in this fantasy world, count me in!

Basically, I want people to think that having some kind of barbecue, clambake, bonfire or limbo contest without me wouldn't be the same, which is technically true. It would be better. But I don't want them to know that!

See, my fear of being seen as the kind of person who's afraid of firecrackers is outpaced only by my fear of firecrackers.

What should I do?

What would our forefathers have done?

Let's keep this between us until I figure it out.

ooo

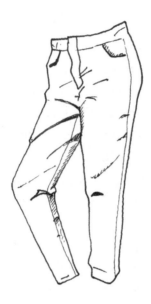

Great New Denim!

The older I get, the more I think life isn't about avoiding pain but surviving it. You can try to outrun life's profoundly upsetting experiences, but sadly, it won't work. Invariably, you'll find yourself at the funeral of a loved one, in the hospital receiving a troubling diagnosis or at a department store trying to buy jeans.

I'd put it off for as long as I could, hoping no one would notice I was wearing the same pair every day. As long as I switch up the shirt, I thought, who's really going to notice? Plus, I do most of my work from home. I'm only around other human beings for a scant few hours each day. For all they know I spend the bulk of my time donning a rich pageant of colorful and varied garb, every hour on the hour choosing a new garment from my plentiful collection of overalls, skorts, culottes, pedal pushers, skirts (both maxi and mini), sarongs, wrap dresses, rompers, jumpers and jorts. For all they know I wear something once and throw it out. For all they know I still keep the notebook I started in high school in which I'd write down what I wore each day, accessories included, to make sure I didn't repeat outfits.

Back when I started that notebook, I had a lot of clothes and not that many friends. These days, I have a lot of friends (who I don't see that often) and not that many clothes.

Actually, I have a lot of clothes. I just don't wear that many of them, which brings me back to the one pair of jeans I wear, the other pair that I used to wear and the rest of the pairs in my closet, which are really just placeholders at this point—a remembrance of jeans past.

Seeing as I hate shopping, I'm always overwhelmed when I head to the department store to rustle up some pants.

But I did it one day. I traveled right into the overly loud Top 40-blaring heart of the beast and rifled through pair after pair of very expensive designer skinny jeans—which is not my preferred cut—in an array of dark and light rinses and waists varying from low-rise to obscenely low.

The jeans and I went to a dressing room. I pulled on a pair. They didn't come up high enough and were too long. I waddled around the room, squinting at myself trying to see whether there was any way that with some altering they'd be worth over 200 bucks.

A very skinny, very fashionable 22-year-old salesgirl knocked on my door to see whether I was finding everything OK, whether I needed any help and whether I was excited about all the "great new denim."

SO EXCITED.

I tried on a few more pairs, which pinched in the wrong places and flared in the wrong places and gave my muffin top a muffin top. And then, defeated and sweaty and feeling as if I'd thrown out my back, I decided life was too short and I would just come back another time when I was in a better mood.

On my way out, as I made my way across the floor, I spied a wall of jeans near the bathroom. I wanted to turn and run away, but something called me over there. I was surprised because some were bootcut and weren't super-extra-low-rise. I looked around confused. What department was this?

It was quieter and calmer than the one I'd been in before. I swiveled my head around trying to figure out if this weird section of clothing tucked off the main floor like an afterthought was for plus sizes or maternity or petite or something—anything—to explain the feeling that I was in a parallel universe. Or Canada. I saw no such signs. And then, a woman who was the opposite of the woman who helped me before was suddenly at my side, chatty and approachable and 60-plus, like your favorite crazy aunt. She was wearing salmon-colored jeans and a lot of bracelets. "The thing with these pants is that they'll stretch a lot, so you really have you get them a size small," she offered.

I took the jeans into a dressing room and put them on. I was stunned. They were super comfortable; they weren't too long; and the waist wasn't too short. It was a little high, to be honest, but for this kind of comfort and style I was on board. I went back out and grabbed a few more pairs. Thank God I had decided to check out this mysterious jeans portal, I thought to myself.

I handed four pairs over the counter to the woman in salmon pants. She found this to be a real hoot. "I love it!" she chirped. "You're like, 'I'm getting my new jeans, and I'm going to be comfortable, and I'm going to look stylish while I'm doing it.'"

Once again, I began to wonder where I was. Were these orthopedic jeans? Geriatric jeans? Pajama jeans?

I stared at the label. "NYDJ. Is that a Nordstrom brand?" I asked hopefully.

"Oh, no. Not Your Daughter's Jeans is a big, big brand," she explained.

My stomach flipped. These were mom jeans. And not shameful mom jeans but loud, proud high-waisted menopausal mom jeans. My excitement over finding jeans I temporarily liked quickly turned to despair. This is why I should always bring a shopping buddy with me, I thought, remembering the time I accidentally tried on men's underwear (don't ask).

I'm still unclear whether the jeans actually looked decent or the hours of trying had scrambled my brain.

I still have them—they're sitting in a bag in my closet—and I keep meaning to try them again and figure out whether to keep them, return them or wear them in 30 years when they're age-appropriate.

In the meantime, I have this one pair I like.

ooo

Am I Not First-Class Material?

I recently flew to New York with "The Adam Carolla Show" to do some dates at Carolines on Broadway. I intended to use the time in the air to get a bunch of work done. However, on the way to my seat I discovered that my co-workers were sitting in first class, while I was sitting in an overhead bin filled with crying children. So I had to spend the rest of the flight time thinking about this injustice.

Am I not first-class material? Am I not fit to enjoy hot nuts and ice cream sundaes and legroom? Do I not deserve to use the first-class bathroom, which is exactly the same as the ones in coach but special because it's in the front?

One of those co-workers was Adam Carolla, who is technically my boss, so it makes sense he'd fly in first. But the other co-worker? He must have used his own money to upgrade to first. Unless there's some way he convinced the company to spring for the ticket. No, there's no way. It had to be his own money. But what if it wasn't?

And so it went for five or so hours, give or take the part where two adorable twin moppets with bronchitis coughed all over me while their mom quietly suggested they cover their mouth. It was vaguely thoughtful but too late. Plus, a life in coach just isn't worth living (I think I read that in the in-flight magazine), so I didn't even try to dodge the sputum.

I'd periodically gaze into first to see some flight attendant kneeling to have a heartfelt face-to-face with a valued passenger. If you ask for something in coach, they basically grimace and throw it at you. I bet they spoon-feed you in first.

By the way, I'm not proud that I'm this petty. I would much prefer not to walk around noticing small inequalities, worrying I'm missing out on some better version of whatever I've received that I could have if only I figure out how to crack the system. It's not my best quality.

My best qualities? I'm funny, empathetic, compassionate, knowledgeable about eyeliner and really good at that carnival game where you have to roll the bowling ball hard enough to get it over the first hump but not so hard that it goes over the second, and I can read street signs from really far away. My worst qualities? I have no sense of direction; I'm conflict-averse; and I go nuts when it comes to planes and hotels. And apartments and where to sit at a restaurant.

Want to know the first thing I do when I check into a hotel room? I ask for a better room. "Hi, do you have a room in which it's possible to walk from one side to the other without having to climb over the bed?" I'll demand like some kind of celebutante or the queen of England.

In college, we had a thing at the end of every year called "room draw," where each student was assigned a random number that determined their order for picking a room for the following year. If two people went in on a two-room double together, the one with the best number selected for the pair. If four went into a quad, an average of the numbers was taken. I remember a friend of mine saying the whole process felt like a calculus problem that, if figured out correctly, could somehow net her her own floor.

Too often, life is like this and I get stuck puzzling over numbers and combinations instead of enjoying the experience or being in the moment. Granted, the flight to New York was a moment I didn't want to be in, but I still suspect I could have handled it in an easier, healthier way.

ooo

I Guess I'm Sick

I am the kind of smug person who never gets sick, which is making the fact that I'm sick right now not only uncomfortable but also baffling. What happened to my superior immune system? My ability to stare down the common cold? My talent for evading influenza?

I sat next to a kid in fourth grade who had the chicken pox and didn't even get it. That's how much I don't get sick.

If sickness had a wanted poster, it would have a picture of *me* on it.

But today? Today, I'm sick. So sick that I'm even thinking of recanting my position on those tissues with lotion in them. "Spare me your slimy tissues!" I used to announce. "And keep your lozenges and Purell, too."

When people would begin to detail the rituals they go through to avoid getting sick, my eyes would glaze over. I could achieve the same, and I didn't have to sleep with a humidifier, gargle echinacea or waterboard myself with Emergen-C. I also didn't get a flu shot, since I hate shots. And before you wag your germy finger at me, I'll just point out that everyone I know is sick and everyone I know gets flu shots.

In fact, my mom got it first, and then my fiancé got it. And since I make out with both of them, it was only a matter of time. Wait! What? That's not what I meant to say.

What I meant to say was because my mom and fiancé hadn't seen each other but I had seen both of them, they decided that I was probably a carrier. I resented their attempts to play "House." Plus, I found it insulting that they would blame me, the healthy person. Is this how you treat someone with a superhuman immune system? They should have been studying and celebrating me, not trying to bring me down to their level with accusations and finger-pointing.

But it's moot because I am now one of you, one of the coughing masses with a headache and runny nose and sore throat and stomachache and allover yucky feeling. And I'm so, so tired. Imagine an elephant that's been kept up for a week—that's how I feel. This isn't very flattering, but I'm just saying, I suspect it's hard to wake up an elephant once it's out. What do you use? A peanut on a stick?

The real kick in the pants is that the plague from which I'm currently trying to recover set up camp on my days off, after I returned from a work trip. My first thought was, I'm lucky I didn't get sick while working because that would have been difficult. I was quick to congratulate my traitorous immune system for, at the very least, its timing. But then I began to resent the fact that I would be spending my days off feeling like crud.

I've had countless conversations with friends that go like this:

Friend: "I'm really sick."

Me: "Maybe you should take a sick day?"

Friend: "No way, I'm saving my sick days for something fun!"

So I guess I'm not alone in wishing I were sick on their time, not mine.

The real question, though, is why now, and why me? Did I need humbling? Was I flying too close to the sun? Was I shining a little too brightly? Was I making others feel less than? Yes to all of them, I hope.

But if you think I'm going to have any sort of new attitude once I recover—if I recover—you're wrong. All I've learned is that flavorologists need to quit churning out new Oreos and instead turn their attention to cough syrup because, holy hell, it's disgusting.

ooo

The Ex Games

I've never really felt self-conscious about having a small chest. It's not that I have a healthy body image; it's that I have an unhealthy one and there are just so many other body parts to worry about that take priority.

But I recently learned that my fiancé's former girlfriend had, let's just say, an ample bosom, and this information is doing all sorts of weird things in my head. For example, I wonder, when he hugs me, does it feel strange? When he spoons me as we sleep, is he thinking there's something missing? When he watches me walk, is there some kind of mental adjustment that must be done to account for lack of jiggle?

And how come he never told me? I don't exactly know how he would have worked it into conversation, but still.

"Maybe that stuff mattered to me when I was a teenager," he tried to explain. "But now it's about how I feel about a person, not how they look," he said, making it worse.

"How wonderful that you like me now that you no longer care about being with someone attractive!" I harrumphed.

As a courtesy, I loudly explained to him what he should have said: The way I am is perfect to him, and he could never imagine wanting anyone else. He said this was true, that he thinks it's a given that I'm attractive and he forgets that I forget.

When people say what you tell them to say, it feels better than you'd think but not as good as if they'd come up with it on their own.

But as I said, I've never really felt self-conscious about having a small chest. This is perhaps because large ones run in my family, and I've watched the kind of brassieres required to keep that situation looking perky—there's a whole lot of underwire and hooks and eyes and straps that dig in. I'm the kind person who occasionally feels that bracelets are confining, who finds layers uncomfortably problematic if the seams don't line up or the sleeves aren't laying flat. So the less that squeezes and digs in and rumples or ripples, the better.

Plus, as someone who grew up overweight and constantly feels there's a fat ghost over her shoulder ready to jump into her body and puff it up, I'm thankful for any part of me being small. To further drive the neurotic point home: Occasionally, I don one of the aforementioned brassieres with the hydraulics and the padding and the lift and the separation—the kind of apparatus that's so uncomfortable I want to rip my hair out and hang myself with it—and then I look in the mirror and turn to the side and wonder whether the fantastic pseudoboobs make me look fat.

So here's the way I found out about the ex-bosoms: Fiancé and I were walking out of a store, and a woman passed us who was leggy and confident and walking with purpose, like someone in deodorant commercial. I asked whether he saw her and said that she's what I imagine his ex looks like. He asked whether I'd ever seen a picture of her, and I said no. I didn't tell him it wasn't for lack of trying. Apparently, she's as private as I am public. I can't get a zit without recording a podcast and writing an article about it, but she isn't even on Facebook.

He said she had a different build than the woman who passed us. I think he intended for that to make me feel better, but I'm more skilled at this game than he is, so I was able to see his "she had wider hips" and raise it to "oh, did she have a big chest?"

He squirmed a little before answering.

I felt bad that I was grilling him. It wasn't coming from a place of jealousy so much as curiosity. But the more he hesitated to tell me about her chest, the more it seemed like he thought this was something that would bump me. And the more he seemed to think it would bump me, the more I wondered whether it should.

This brings us to today. I'm still wondering how to feel about it. I suppose it doesn't really matter because his past is his past, and how I feel about it won't change anything.

But still.

ooo

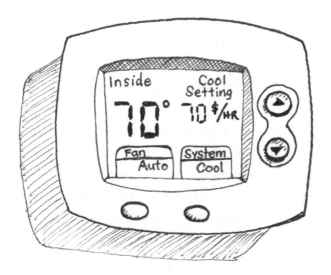

Post-Traumatic Electric Bill Syndrome

L ast night my fiancé did something that tested the limits of my love for him and caused me to wonder whether our entire relationship is built on a foundation of lies. I'm talking about a transgression so great I never could have seen it coming because I'd never expect this kind of monstrous act from someone I trust. Or rather, trusted.

He turned off the air conditioning.

I stared at him like he was insane. I tried to talk sense into him, but he couldn't hear me over the sweat pooling in his ears. And then, he made an announcement that will haunt me till the end of my days, that functioned like a shot across the bow and should have been made in a beer hall. "From now on, let's try not to run the air conditioning and instead open the windows," he said.

I've never felt less attracted to someone.

The way I see it, outside is hot and unpleasant and full of bugs; inside is cool and pleasant and full of Twitter and cable TV. Killing the air conditioning is bad enough, but why would you then go and remove the one thing that keeps the outside out and the inside in?

Why not just invite a rapist over for dinner? Or drive the wrong way down a one-way street? Or dip yourself in honey, roll yourself in bacon and hang out in an area heavily populated by bears while doing things known to anger them, like poking them, making comments about their women or yelling, "Aha! I knew it!" when they relieve themselves in the woods?

I mean, I do understand where this God-awful idea comes from. It's post-traumatic stress from the sight of our last electric bill. Turns out cooling our apartment costs roughly the same as sending a small child to private school. But we don't yet have any small children, and we never will if this continues. In this heat, the feeling of my flesh touching itself is enough to make me nuts, let alone the feeling of someone else's.

But I'm not one to complain, as you can probably tell, and so far, I've discovered that if I either stand still or stand still in front of the open refrigerator and freezer, it isn't so bad. The food is rotting, but there are casualties in all wars.

The challenge to living without air conditioning is moving around, showering, doing anything more to my hair than wrapping a symbolic white towel around it and, of course, sleeping. It's impossible to sleep without a lot of cold air blowing on me, which is confounding on many levels. The heat makes me sleepy but unable to actually sleep. If you're looking for a way to wake up angry, cranky and frizzy, I recommend turning off the air conditioning.

It occurs to me that in a way, I'm extorting money from my fiancé by becoming so unpleasant and shiny that he'll be left with no choice but to turn on the air conditioning.

That's the goal, at least.

ooo

About That Time I Test-Drove a Car Into Another Car

Something horrible happened to me at a car dealership, and I'm not just talking about the experience of being at a car dealership. No, I'm talking about something so awful, embarrassing, confidence-crushing and possibly criminal that I intended to leave the dealership and never speak of it again. I then planned to change my name and number, leave my loved ones and live out my days in a small yurt in Central Asia, far away from cars and the people who sell them.

But that seems like a lot of work, and I'm kind of lazy, not to mention really bad at secrets. So here I am, humbly asking that you not judge me for what I'm about to reveal.

Recently, while test-driving a brand-new car, I kinda sorta backed into another brand-new car.

Allow me to explain. I'd been car shopping for a while, and I was pretty familiar with the whole test-drive rigmarole. I expected this one to be no different than the others. I would show up, make awkward small talk with someone who is curiously unable to answer the most basic questions about options and packages, go on a comically short drive around the dealership, hitting a max speed of about 30 mph, be pressured into sitting at a desk and talking numbers, even though I'm not ready to make a decision, and then receive a call from this person between two and five times a week for the rest of my life.

Also, I'd catch a whiff of the dealer's cologne and wonder for the rest of the day how he could have so strongly imbued the air around my nose with his scent—which feels like an aromatic violation—in such a short time.

So, my fiancé and I show up at the dealership on this day, and instead of making a copy of my license, the dealer literally throws me a set of keys, like we're buddies in a cop movie, and says, "Let's drive!"

The car I'm test-driving is brand-new—so new that all the upholstery still has plastic film covering. I assume the dealer will remove it, so I can experience the car without feeling like I'm driving Dexter's kill room, but he doesn't. After the aforementioned short slow test drive, we drive back onto the lot. Instead of saying, "Just stop anywhere, and I'll park it," as I've come to expect, he suggests I back it into any available space so I can experience the backup camera.

"Are you sure?" I ask, more than once.

"Sure!" he trills. "If you're comfortable with it."

I'm not really, but I defer to his can-do attitude, deciding in that moment that I've been selling myself short. Who knows how many experiences and opportunities I've missed out on because I'm holding myself back? Well, no more. Yesterday's me wouldn't park the car. But today's me? She's parking!

"Actually, why don't you back into that one up there," he says pointing to a smaller and narrower space a little further down. "Then you can see the car side by side last year's model."

This is definitely a bad idea, but his positive attitude is so contagious! As I back into the space—a parking maneuver I never use in real life, as will soon be apparent—I look at the backup camera with all its lines and squiggles. Indecipherable! Then I look up to make sure I'm not too close to the car in front of me, which doesn't even make sense, and then I hear the sickening sound of metal scraping on metal.

"Did I just hit a car?" I ask, as if through a mouthful of vomit. "Yes," say both the dealer and my fiancé.

Now look. Obviously, I'm the one piloting the car like a drunk 4-year-old, but how did the other two people in the vehicle, who presumably were witnessing the slow-speed collision, not give me a heads up or a warning or a "HEY, YOU'RE ABOUT TO HIT THAT CAR"?

"You seemed awfully close, but I thought you knew what you were doing," said my fiancé. I responded: "I NEVER know what I'm doing! Never assume I know what I'm doing!"

Then the dealer piped up: "Don't worry about it. I didn't see anything. I promise I didn't see anything."

I gingerly got out of the car. I looked around for cameras, convinced I was about to be arrested. Then I thought about how frequently these cars are driven. "This must happen a lot, right?" I asked, hopefully.

"Actually, this is only the second time it's happened in 10 years," the dealer chirped. He asked us to come back to his desk and have a seat. On the way, he got pulled aside to deal with another customer, at which point I realized that I pretty much had to leave right then because nothing good was going to happen if I stuck around. I hastily made up a reason why I had to leave but gave the dealer my phone number.

He called me once, and I nearly wet myself when I saw his number pop up on my phone. But he was just curious whether I was interested in the car, which I wasn't. He didn't say anything about a "you break it, you buy it" policy, which is what I was afraid of.

I mostly take this experience as a sign the universe wants me to be chauffeured.

ooo

Clutter, Memory and the Junk in My Car

Yesterday, I sold the car I've had—and hated—for the last 15 years. Instead of feeling relieved and happy, like I would have expected, I just feel numb, weird and a little empty. It's not that I miss that hunk of metal with its fading paint, steering wheel the size of a small Hula-Hoop and top-of-the-line single-CD player. On the contrary, I'm happy to be free of those things. It's just that after 15 years, I formed a relationship with the car—an unhealthy and annoying one, the kind your friends tell you to get out of—and apparently, it got under my skin.

I wish I were one of those people who embraced change. If I were, I would be sipping tea in Jakarta and running my fingers through my freshly cropped hair while waiting for Ernesto, the man who's helping me get my pilot license and with whom I'm having a torrid affair, to arrive and whisk me away for an afternoon of flight lessons and romance. "Don't get attached, Ernesto," I'd murmur at 20,000 feet. At that height he probably wouldn't hear me though, so I'd have to yell it.

"DON'T GET ATTACHED, ERNESTO!" I'd yell.

"Don't touch the latch?" he'd ask. If we didn't meet an untimely demise in a fiery crash due to me trying to warn him I'm no good, then I'd likely break his heart later when I'd pick up and move to another exotic locale and changed my hair again, as is my way.

I wish I were like that—capricious and whimsical. Instead, I'm a flightless creature of habit with the same hairstyle since high school and a penchant for clutter.

You know those people who can't make attachments? Those people who can love and leave, pick up and go, cut and run? Rambling men, mostly? I'm the opposite. It's as if my heart is made of suction cups and my hands are lint rollers and the rest of my body is made of something else very sticky. Velcro? Balloons? Dog noses? And so, I become a little attached to anything I come in contact with. It's for this reason I have trouble throwing things away. I'm an emotional hoarder. And possibly a regular hoarder.

Part of the emotional wallop of saying goodbye to the car I'd longed to be rid of was cleaning it out before the buyer came. It was very similar to that feeling you always have when moving—looking around at a place that is so imbued with you and thinking, "In just 24 hours, this will no longer look like this, and it will no longer be mine." And your mind reels at how this can be, not to mention the fact that you should have started packing weeks ago. And then the process of moving in and getting comfortable is experienced in reverse as you begin taking things off the walls and putting all your belongings in boxes. By the time the moving men come the next day the apartment no longer looks like the place you knew, the place where you experienced all the memories that came flooding back to you as you were packing. It looks the same as when you moved in: cold and impersonal, as if you'd never been there. It's all kind of jarring.

I bought the car in 1998, shortly after a friend died. I was deeply in mourning, and that sadness always clung to the car. As I was cleaning it out, I found all sorts of stuff from that time of my life: a birth announcement for my friend's daughter, who's now a teenager, a laminate for the 5th anniversary party of the magazine where I worked, stickers and flyers for the band I played in. At the time, I didn't know what to do with myself or my stuff, so I stashed it in my car and tried not to feel anything.

As the family who bought the car was driving away, I stood at the window watching, thinking it would be the last time I saw the car so I ought to commit it to memory. After about 10 minutes, the car came back to return the sunglasses I'd left inside. They were sunglasses I didn't want, ones that I bought while in the depths of mourning when I was having trouble not bursting into tears.

I think there's a lesson in here about clutter and memory and the passage of time—and maybe about what happens when you don't finish processing everything.

The truth is, I'm still trying to figure it out.

ooo

Employment History, Vol. 1

In honor of recently celebrating Labor Day, I thought I'd take a look back at some of the highlights of my rich work history. But then I realized I'd rather look at the lows, as there are more of them and, frankly, I think I'm still pissed.

In high school, my friend Jen referred me for a babysitting job. One young kid, convenient location, good hours. I was surprised she didn't want it for herself, and soon I found out why. Shortly after meeting the adorable toddler and his mother, who needed someone to watch him while she had permanent makeup tattooed on her face, which I assume was a response to an acrimonious divorce, I discovered the kid had two pastimes about which he was equally passionate: "Barney & Friends" and biting people. To be honest, this wasn't first time I'd be been bitten by a child. When I was about 4 or 5 years old and "Jaws" was all the rage, my family took a trip to Lake Tahoe. As so often happens when you're a kid, I began playing with the other children at the swimming pool. (Have you noticed that dogs gravitate toward one another and children gravitate toward one another but adults do not? It's curious.) Soon, one of the kids put her hands above her head to approximate a fin, hummed the "Jaws" theme and chomped down on my shoulder. So I guess what I'm trying to say is that I had relevant experience for this particular job. Worse than the biting, though, was the Barney. It's been over 20 years, but just typing the words has put the song back in my head.

Soon after, I began working as a greeter at the defunct music store Sam Goody. Theoretically, this involved saying "Hi! Welcome to Sam Goody" as people entered and "Bye! Thank you for shopping at Sam Goody" as they left. But in reality it meant shouting "Hi! Welcome t—" and "Bye! Thank you for sh—" at people's backs. It also involved an aggressive pat down every time you left the store, and a manager who repeatedly admonished, "Alison, help the customers," even though they'd already declined my (little) help. "Ask them again," she'd hiss. Frankly, between being accosted by a manic greeter and being asked repeatedly whether you need help finding anything, shopping at Sam Goody was probably an unpleasant experience. I'd like to think I had a hand in that.

Fast-forward a great many years, through working at a coffee cart that required me to wear white—the hardest color to keep clean and the most difficult substance to keep off your clothing (or maybe I'm just messy)—interviewing men dressed up as giant vegetables, working for an editor who demanded to know how many pounds of tomatoes are used a year by all the chefs in New York City (when I tried to explain why it's impossible to ascertain this number at 5 p.m. on a Friday, I was seen as "difficult," an injustice that to this day makes me want to throw a shoe) dancing on live TV and a brief experience with temping.

About the temp job: I started on Monday and called in sick on Wednesday and quit on Friday. I never quite understood what it was the company did, partly because I was warned by a woman who wrote her name all over her chair in Wite-Out not to ask too many questions. I think it had something to do with list maintenance for a company that sent spam.

I remember sitting down at the desk of the woman who was to train me and noticing her computer was festooned with pictures of a calico cat. I held off asking the cat's name because I wanted to ration out possible conversation topics. (I later found out it was named Venti because she "loved Starbucks.")

She handed me a few sheets of paper stapled together titled "Rules for Doing Something or Other." "This is basically what we do here," she said, running her hand over the outline. I seriously considered the possibility that "what we do here" was make outlines.

And then, some tall guy with floppy hair entered the building, and all the women swooned. His name was Blaine. He did tai chi in the park, and he'd designed the barely functioning software we used to maintain the lists. In my brief tenure, I would be told no less than 17 times that Blaine designed the software, each time the person giving a faraway look that began to frighten me.

But the real problem was there were two of us assigned to do the job of half a monkey, and the boredom was soul-crushing. Up to this point, I'd wondered where the jobs were that paid you to sit around doing nothing. I'd found one, and I hated it.

Upon reflection, I fear I come off as an asshole with a poor work ethic, which I assure you is a mischaracterization. Never mind that I characterized myself.

Now, if you'll excuse me, I have to perform a Barneyectomy on myself before I walk into traffic.

ooo

I'm Turning Into a Dog-Pageant Mom

My dog has tested out of level 1 agility and into level 2, which means two things: I'm very proud of him and I'm worried I'm going to become one of *those people*. In case you're unfamiliar with the notion of *those people*, they are the ones who get so sucked into a way of life they cease to have any self-awareness or shame.

I'm reminded of the time my fiancé bought us season passes to Disneyland.

"We just have to be careful we don't become *those people*," I whispered as a couple in matching denim shirts with Mickey and Minnie patches walked by.

Some other people I don't want to become? The people who talk your ear off about Pilates, the people who enjoy line dancing, the people who scrapbook, the people who knit, the people who are obsessed with "Harry Potter" or "Twilight" and the people who are afraid of their microwave.

Lest you are one of those people and feel judged, let me remind you that for a good year I was obsessed with the Panda Cam and I recently enrolled in a frozen-dinner rewards program through which, if I play my cards right, I might get a set of matching mugs. Speaking of cards, one of my greatest regrets is that I've never been able to pull off any sort of fancy card shuffling. You know that move where you're shuffling and you pull your hands apart and then slam them back together and the cards look like an accordion? I tried to master that till my fingers were raw. So what I'm trying to say is, I'm not exactly cool.

But back to *those people*. I'm destined to become one because I come from a long line of them: My dad collects stamps (he tried to instill a passion for philately in his children, but it never stuck). My sister and her husband collect squished pennies and keep them in a special squished-penny holder. And my mom, though svelte, knows everything there is to know about jelly beans. It's only natural I'd become an enthusiast. Maybe I shouldn't fight it.

The way dog agility works is there are all sorts of obstacles set up in the room, ramps and tunnels and hurdles and whatnot, and as a class you take turns leading your dog through the individual obstacles. At the end, you put it all together. Some dogs stop halfway up a ramp, refuse to go through a tunnel or go around the hurdle instead of over. Other dogs, like mine, though younger and littler than the rest, take to it instantly and are fearless and really seem to enjoy it. This elicits a ton of praise from the instructors, which fills empty spots in me I didn't know I had. After class, my dog and I walk around puffed up and proud of ourselves. People compliment my dog, and I accept the compliments as if I gave birth to him or had anything to do with his unusual talent. And then, we come home; he takes a nap; and I look at him and smile and fantasize about ribbons. What has become of me?

Thankfully, there are little impediments along the way that will hopefully prevent me from turning into a full-fledged dog-pageant mom. For example, everyone at the dog gym (yes, you read that right) where I take Oliver wears a fanny pack filled with treats. They refer to these as "feed bags," but to my eyes they are fanny packs. Mine is a fanny not enhanced by the addition of a pack, so I carry treats around in a Ziploc bag, and once a class I accidentally drop the bag and all the treats spill on the floor.

I guess I'll be getting a fanny pack—because I'm one of *those people* now.

ooo

I Can't Stop Thinking About Crying Baby Elephants

Y ou know that feeling when there's something delicious in your house that you're trying not to eat but you can't get it out of your head? Eventually, you get to a point where you realize you have to either eat it or throw it out because you won't get any peace as long as it's around. (Please tell me you relate, even if it's a lie.)

This is how I feel right now, only it isn't a forbidden carbohydrate that's calling my name. It's a link I'm trying not to click. Specifically, it's the one that will take me to the news story currently making rounds on the internet about a baby elephant in China that cried for five hours after being attacked and rejected by its mother. You may have already seen or heard about it. All I know is I went to sleep one night blissfully unaware that elephants produce tears and woke up to nonstop baby elephant chatter. If I had a nickel for every well-meaning person who emailed or tweeted me the link, I'd have close to a dollar. (You know, we really need to adjust that phrase for inflation.)

The point is I don't want to read this story. I don't want to feel the sadness it will make me feel. You know that scene in "Dumbo" where he's a baby and his mother is rocking him in her trunk and everyone is crying, especially me? That scene wrecked me. Years of therapy can't remove that image from my memory, and it wasn't even real.

OK, fine. I just clicked the link.

I couldn't help myself! I'm powerless in the face of baby animals that are experiencing strong emotions! And then I told myself that I definitely wasn't going to try to find video footage of the crying elephant ... while trying to find video footage of the crying elephant because I was curious as to what an elephant's wails sound like. Apparently, seeing a photo of its puffy red eyes and wet trunk wasn't enough. "But what if the video contains footage of the mother stomping the baby?" I wondered. A nervous flutter went through me. Most of me didn't want to see that, but there was a tiny bit of me that was sort of curious, and I'm disturbed that part is in me. (Mercifully, I didn't find anything.)

I'm confused by this compulsion to watch and read things that will make me experience a cocktail of emotions I'm trying to avoid. I think on some level I actually do want to feel these feelings—ones I'm repressing in my daily life—and these stories act like little emotional-release valves.

The other day, I thought it would be a good idea to watch videos of people with cochlear implants hearing for the first time after a lifetime of deafness. Have you seen these videos? Instant tears. I don't mean the kind of thing where you see it and then think about it for a second and then tear up. I mean you're watching and the person in the video starts crying and before you can even process what's happening, you're a puddle.

I've always somewhat harshly judged the people who enjoy brutal, gruesome or excessively violent videos and movies. I'm talking about the people who love torture porn franchises like "Saw" or "Hostel" and pass around YouTube videos of beheadings; and to a lesser degree, the "Tosh.0" audience that enjoys countless clips of people falling and getting hurt. To my imagination, these viewers are watching and either feeling nothing or, worse, laughing at the misfortune of others. I'm beginning to wonder whether I haven't judged them too harshly.

Maybe they aren't bloodless automatons but people playing their own version of emotional Russian roulette, trying to see how much they can tolerate. Maybe they're afraid of their own emotional reactions and trying to practice tamping them down, an understandably desirable skill in a culture that values stoicism.

To be clear: Watching videos and movies with which you identify and empathize (we're all that baby elephant) is not the same as watching something in which the victim is objectified. But I'm beginning to wonder whether the desire to view both doesn't come from a similar place inside—trying to learn to release and restrict our own unmanageable emotions.

ooo

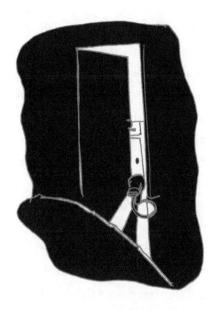

When Hair Dryers Attack

The other day, my hair dryer attacked me, which is the closest thing to a loved one's betrayal I've ever experienced.

Here's what happened: Like all reasonable women, I have two hair dryers. There's the expensive heavy one, which must somehow work better because I paid so much for it, and the cheapo portable one I bought at the drugstore, which is my emergency backup and travel dryer. To spice things up and infuse some whimsy into my otherwise predictable life, one day at home, I decided to dry my hair with the cheapo one. Just to keep my hair guessing. I was kind of blown away by how well it worked (no pun intended). Don't tell Vidal, but I daresay, I preferred it to the other one. And then something happened. I typically leave it out when telling this story. However, I will tell you because I think you deserve the whole truth.

As regular readers know, I have an adorable dog. What you don't know is he loves the hair dryer. When I use it, he sits at my feet, basking in the stream of air. I think he likes the warmth. It's also possible he just hates the natural look. So after blow-drying my hair and observing the aforementioned improved volume and shine, I pointed the dryer at my dog and we cavorted in our usual way: him facing the stream of air and doing this thing where he tips his head up and squints, which looks like he's either farting or smiling, while I repeatedly ask, "Who's a good boy?" (Hint: He is!)

Then I worried, as I always do, that maybe the air is too warm, even though he seems to like it. So I thought I'd press the "cool shot" button. I'm pretty sure this would be the first time in the history of hair drying someone has deliberately sought out this button. For those unfamiliar, the "cool shot" button is a button that, in the fantasy world of hair dryer literature—the literature you find on the box the dryer came in and in women's magazines—helps you "lock in style" with a blast of cool air. In the real world of my bathroom, this button doesn't lock in anything other than an extra 10 minutes of my time. If you ever find yourself thinking, "Why is the hair dryer making a lot of noise but no heat is coming out and my hair isn't getting dry?" congrats, you've found the cool shot button. The annoying thing about the button, other than the fact that it doesn't work, is it's always right where your hand naturally rests while holding the dryer, so it's easy to press accidentally. At least that's the case with my expensive dryer. I was having trouble finding it on the cheapo one, so I flipped the dryer around to get a good look. I was leaning forward over the dryer, and the dryer was in my right hand. Suddenly, I felt a tug on the right side of my head. It was sucking in my hair. My hair was wrapped around the spinning fan inside the contraption, and more and more was being pulled in.

I tried to turn the dryer off, but because I don't use it frequently, I accidentally pushed the button as far as it would go, from "low" to "off" to "high." The dryer roared and pulled my hair in faster. Panicked, I pushed the slider back in the other direction—"high" to "off" to "low." This wasn't going as planned. The third attempt worked, and I managed to turn it off. And then, with one hand holding the dryer, since letting go would mean the weight of the dryer yanking my hair out, I went to the mirror to appraise the damage.

It was as I expected: My hand was attached to the dryer, which was attached to my hair, which was attached to my head. I reached across my face and grabbed the dryer with my left hand and tried to loosen the hair with my right, since I'm right-handed. I couldn't see over my arms. I was like a one-person game of human vs. hair dryer Twister. The hair wasn't budging. I grabbed the nearest scissors—manicure scissors—and debated cutting myself free. I was hot and sweaty and panicked, and the dryer, ironically light and flimsy, was beginning to feel like an anchor. I decided I wasn't ready to resort to such a drastic measure, I tried to slip the manicure scissors off my fingers, but then I realized they were stuck. I felt like a giant trapped in a 6-pound bowling ball. And now I couldn't even call anyone because one hand was holding the dryer and the other looked like the last prop made by a hard-of-hearing prop master on "Edward Scissorhands" shortly before he was fired.

I finally pried the scissors off by using the edge of the counter. I then did something handy: found a screwdriver and, using my left hand, unscrewed all four screws holding the dryer together. It took quite a bit longer than you might expect, since "righty tighty, lefty loosey" loses all meaning in a mirror. And then I tried to pull the hair dryer open to save my precious tresses, but it wouldn't budge. I'd spent what felt like an hour unscrewing the damn thing, but its molded plastic body wasn't opening. And that's when I gave up, imprisoned my fingers in the scissors once more and cut myself free.

I'm not sure who to blame for my fiasco, but I'm open to suggestions.

ooo

Candy Crushed

I should probably delete Candy Crush from my phone. I'm not going to, but I probably should. Here's why:

The other day while having a conversation with my sister, I found myself wishing I could reach across the space between us, place my index finger on her left eye and my thumb on her right eye and squish them together until they exploded and disappeared. Sadly, this isn't even a move in Candy Crush, though it's similar to one. For it to really work, her eyes would have to be made of candy, and she would need to have at least three. I also long to group trees, cars and buildings into groups of three or—be still my heart—groups of four and slam them together to make them disappear.

It's not that I'm destructive. It's that I'm obsessed.

For the uninitiated, Candy Crush, or Candy Crush Saga (its full name), is a superpopular game that its makers refer to as "an addictive and delicious puzzle adventure." It's made by King.com, a British company that's currently the top supplier of games to Facebook and Apple (it surpassed Zynga, maker of Words With Friends and other popular games, in June) and is worth somewhere between $5 billion and $7 billion.

I'm not really a big video game person or puzzle person. In fact, I can think of nothing more deadly boring than a big jigsaw puzzle spread out in a zillion pieces on an empty table. To me, jigsaw puzzles have always been something you do to pass the time when you have absolutely zero better options.

I can imagine someone saying: "You guys go ahead to prom. I'll just stay here and work on this 1,000-piece puzzle of a kitten."

Or "No, you guys go ahead to the amusement park. I'm under house arrest, and the electricity has gone out, so I'm going to drink cold Postum and work on this 2,000-piece jigsaw puzzle of a dandelion."

Or "Hot air ballooning? I couldn't possibly go hot air ballooning with you. I am paralyzed from the waist down and have contracted scabies, so I'm just going to stay home, break in these new pajamas, scratch myself and put the finishing touches on this 3,000-piece puzzle of, get this, a hot air balloon!"

In terms of time wasters, I'm more of an '80s sitcom and mess-around-on-Twitter person. Sometimes I'll spend an hour or two looking for something I've misplaced. But at some point while hearing my fiancé talk to my mom about how much money the makers of Candy Crush have raked in, and how he refuses to download the app because he's convinced it's somehow so persuasive that it convinces otherwise-sensible people to part with tons of money to keep playing, I decided I would take that challenge. It's sort of the online equivalent of being compelled to take a drug after watching an after-school special.

So far, I haven't fallen into financial ruin or sold an organ on the black market to keep playing. The only negative consequence of allowing Candy Crush into my life—I mean, other than wanting to squish my sister's eyes—is that it's functioning like a gateway drug, and I need something stronger. Candy is dandy, but strip clubs and murder might be more my speed. Do I dare dip a toe into the world of "Grand Theft Auto V"? My co-workers have discussed looking at their calendars and making sure they didn't have anything they really needed to get done before purchasing the game. Unfortunately, once again, I see this as a challenge. Other than a ton of work and planning a wedding, I think I'm wide open!

So, talk to you in a few months?

ooo

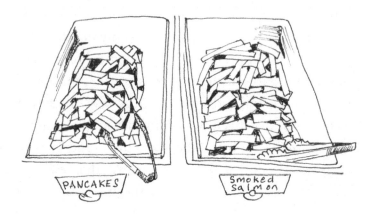

Sleepless in Portland

Have you ever had one of those days where you're convinced you didn't sleep a wink and the only way you know you actually did is because you dreamed? And not even about anything cool, like finding a door that leads to a roller coaster in the back of your closet, but about something prosaic, like trying to find a parking spot?

That's the kind of night I had recently at an exceedingly hip hotel in Portland, Oregon, which, decorwise, was somewhere between dorm room, white-collar prison and depressing flophouse that men who are going through a divorce in their 50s move into. The room had a mattress a few inches off the floor, a sink a few inches from the bed, high ceilings, a molded plastic chair, paper-thin walls and a record player. Lord knows only maniacs would dream of traveling without their vinyl collection. It also had small-batch artisanal everything, including soda made with real cane sugar in the minibar. This really bummed me out; I would have killed for a Diet Coke.

Anyway, for whatever reason—and I'm not saying it was the five cups of coffee I drank to get my energy up before performing with Adam Carolla at the Aladdin Theater earlier that evening—I tossed and turned all night, woke up in the worst mood ever and began to despair over how I was possibly going to drag myself through the next few days.

If you are in that phase of life during which sleep comes easy but is somewhat optional, take advantage of it. Stay awake from ages 19 to 23 because no one tells you that one day you won't feel like yourself for at least a year, possibly two, because you made the mistake of taking a red-eye.

I used to pull all-nighters by choice. It was my preferred method for meeting deadlines. And then I'd sleep for a couple hours, wake up refreshed and go about my day. I was so springy in my youth. Now I'm brittle and cranky. It takes me longer and longer to wake up, and longer and longer to go to sleep. Eventually, I'll just wake up and begin getting ready for bed.

Back to Portland, where I picked myself up off the floor, took a lukewarm shower in a claw-foot bathtub, washed my hair with what I'm pretty sure was body wash and then made my way down to the breakfast room. (A word about claw-foot tubs: I realize they're kitschy and cool, but I'm never excited to use one. And conversely, I've never seen a big modern shower and found myself disappointed with the ease with which I would be bathing.)

I was hoping to grab some coffee to go, but they didn't have to-go cups. As I was processing this news, I ran into Adam—or at least I think it was him. On a good day, it now takes a while for my eyes to adjust. But this wasn't a good day. I faced the familiar human-shaped blur in front of me and tried to focus. I felt as if I'd been packed in rock salt and left to brine overnight. My eyelids were so puffy I may as well have been looking through two bagels. Then I tried to speak, but my voice sounded like the noise that comes out of one of those big coffee thermoses when it's empty and you tip it forward and pump desperately.

"Did you sleep? I didn't sleep," I bleated.

There was a time when I wished to come across as a little more easygoing and delightful, but now I was just angry that the hotel didn't provide box springs.

I surveyed the food-shaped blobs in front of me. Adam warned me that what he mistook for "pancake shards" were actually slices of smoked fish. I felt better knowing I wasn't the only one whose senses waited a solid few hours to kick in.

After eating everything that wasn't nailed down—the only way to survive a sleepless night—drinking too much coffee and taking a two-hour nap, which really meant an hour and 50 minutes of playing Candy Crush, setting my alarm for 10 minutes and then getting under the covers and closing my eyes, I began to feel more like myself.

And sadly, by that I mean feel old.

ooo

The Worst Kind of Flirt

There are world-class flirts, and then there are world-class flirts. I'm not one of them. I'm regional at best, and a very small region at that. Like my house. I was thinking about this recently because I had an interaction with someone who's known in my circle to be the kind of guy who everyone—women, men, married women and men, household pets—has crushes on.

I'd met him before and had some brief interactions, but I never quite understood what all the fuss was about. He struck me as warm and cute, but loads of people fit that description. And that was before a recent exchange where, in the course of talking to me, he grabbed the tip of my index finger gently between his thumb and index finger, held it for a few seconds, looked into my eyes and said, "I know" in response to something I'd said. It was the strangest gesture—who grabs the tip of your finger? Yet it was so oddly intimate and sincere that I had to look around to make sure we were still in a crowded room and my clothes were still on.

It was then I began to realize he's the best—or worst, depending on how you look at it—kind of flirt there is: the kind who isn't doing it intentionally and probably isn't even aware of its effect. He likely goes about his day in a haze of fingertip holding and eye contact, which to him is just being friendly, oblivious to all the little connections people feel they're forging with him. Because that's what flirtation is: an isolated transcendent moment of connection that means something to one person and nothing to the other. I think I read that on a needlepoint.

Were I 12 or 13 years old, an age when attracting a member of the opposite sex seemed an impossible feat despite my myriad jelly bracelets, bi-level hair and homemade Michael Jackson buttons, that one moment would have probably launched me into a yearslong crush. From ages 8 to 13, I had it bad for a guy I'd only had a few conversations with one summer at tennis camp. He was older, and we were paired up to be a doubles team. He told me he noticed that when I was up at the net and got scared, I would sometimes close my eyes. He said that maybe that wasn't the best strategy. He *got* me!

Then he went back to his life, and I went back to mine. I'm sure he didn't give me a second thought. I thought about him all the time—every time I blew out birthday candles or threw coins into a fountain or played MASH. It was a spectacular day when I walked into the first meeting of drama club as a freshman in high school and there he was. I couldn't believe my good fortune. Fate had clearly brought us back together! I asked him whether he could give me a ride home one day. He was a senior and had his own car. I quickly called my mom to tell her I'd found my own way home. I had big plans. This almost qualified as a date!

On the ride home, I reminded him of our shared tennis camp past. I'm not sure what I was expecting. A high five and a marriage proposal? He said he remembered the camp and thought he remembered me but wasn't sure. Things weren't going as I'd hoped. Then he dropped me off and asked a junior to the winter formal.

In the course of telling this story, I was struck by my own naive hopefulness. I had so much to learn—about everything.

And though in time I became a little more discriminating, I never really did learn how to flirt.

ooo

On Being Indirect

I've been on this planet for more than two decades but fewer than four, and only lately have I come to realize how many years I've spent communicating in a way that's remarkably indirect. For example, see the previous sentence. But I've also noticed that instead of asking my fiancé whether he will do something around the house, I merely announce that a thing needs doing. It's incredibly annoying and possibly passive-aggressive. It's not one of my finer qualities (which include my hair, compassion and knowledge of "The Facts of Life" trivia).

For example, instead of saying: "Honey, could I ask you a favor? Would you mind taking the trash out?" I will instead proclaim, as if to an imaginary coterie of servants and trash fairies, "The trash is ready to go out."

And instead of saying, "Could you take the puppy out?" I will announce, as if answering a question no one asked, "The dog probably needs a walk."

And when we dine on the couch in front of the television—because we are civilized—and I realize we've forgotten paper towels and don't feel like using my T-shirt as a napkin, instead of saying, "Could you grab a couple paper towels?" I will simply pose the following brainteaser: "Are there any paper towels in here?"

If I were him, I would have dumped my ass ages ago. And I would have been indirect about that, too. I'd say: "This relationship is ready to be over. A breakup could happen."

The crazy thing is that while I recognize I'm coming off as demanding, that isn't my intention. It's actually quite the opposite. I'm trying to be polite and trying not to make him feel like he has do these chores, because I'm perfectly capable of doing them myself. It's more like I'm just giving him the option of doing them. I'm giving him first right of refusal.

But because my fiancé is a people-pleaser, when I phrase something in this oblique manner he pops up from the couch—albeit probably a little resentful—to do whatever it is he thinks I'm hinting I want him to do.

This really isn't the dynamic I'm trying to create, though I appreciate the bounty of Bounty.

I don't know why phrasing things in a direct manner comes so unnaturally to me. I don't know whether it's because I grew up with parents who are even more indirect than I am. Or maybe it's because I want to get along. Perhaps I'm afraid of being perceived as bossy.

This last one is a real detriment when it comes to actual work situations. I recently emailed an assistant to ask whether he had a certain person's contact information. He replied: "Nope. Sorry."

I was stunned.

Did he really think I was idly inquiring whether he had this contact info? I was asking him to track it down and send it to me.

Instead of going down the road I was headed—angry about the lack of respect I felt I was being shown—I made a decision right then and there that the best way to handle this henceforth would be to just spell it out, to say: "Do you have so-and-so's contact info? If not, could you track it down? Thanks."

The thing is, I feel like I should have figured this out ages ago.

So I ask you: Am I alone in struggling with this? Are you comfortable expressing exactly what you want in personal and professional life? And if so, how did you arrive at that? And how do I catch up?

It'd be nice if someone left some comments.

ooo

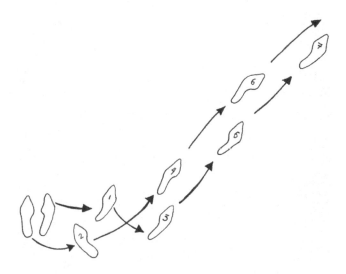

I Do Not Enjoy Dancing

I do not enjoy dancing. I don't want to shake my groove thang, get down on it, boogie-woogie, cut a rug, trip the light fantastic, do the hustle, get out on the dance floor and show 'em how it's done, do the mash potato, stomp!, twerk or lambada. I've been immunized against disco fever. The rhythm has yet to get me.

You know how some people feel alive when they're dancing? That's how I feel when I'm not dancing.

I'm never more in touch with my spirit animal than when I'm at a wedding and everyone is dancing and I'm sitting at a table eating cake at a glacial pace and pretending to be engrossed in my phone. I usually follow this maneuver with a slow saunter to the restroom to kill more time. If I have to check a voicemail while I'm in there? Jackpot!

I wish I weren't this way. I wish I weren't "Footloose" before Kevin Bacon arrived because I think it suggests I'm locked up and probably frigid. Dancing is about sensuality and celebration and something primal that is greater than you and me. I wish I could tap into this on the dance floor and lose myself in the music and give myself over to the moment. Instead, I usually just don't know what to do with my purse or my hands. And I never know if I'm moving my head too much or too little. I am the opposite of fluid.

It hasn't always been this way. I took tap, ballet and jazz as a youngster. I was one of the featured mice in a performance of "Three Blind Mice." I wore a tail and everything. And I also suffered through cotillion, which is an outdated form of social torture disguised as ballroom dance classes enjoyed by the children of pretentious debutantes.

So I should be set, right?

I'm OK with slow dancing. It's perilous for my dance partner, seeing as I'm fantastically uncoordinated and I will likely step on his toes at one point or another. But at least when it comes to slow dancing I know the moves. It's fast cool-people dancing that overwhelms me. I just don't know how to look cool doing it. And don't tell me it isn't about looking cool. You know all that stuff I said about losing yourself in the moment and feeling the beat and becoming a conduit for the music and the emotion and all that? It's also about looking cool.

There was a time when I would hit the dance floor and show off my craaaaaazy dances, which happen to be The Roger Rabbit and The Mashed Potato. Of course, I was doing these ironically with a sort of "Hey, you guys. Look at me pretending to be the kind of person who would do these dances" look on my face. At a certain point, I realized there is no such thing as ironic dancing, and from far away you are just that person who is doing these dances. I'm not sure how I feel about that person.

I've asked my friends who love to dance what it is that appeals to them because the whole thing is beginning to feel like a paradox.

After pushing through a lot of "I don't know. ... I just love it," I discovered that one of my super-cool-on-the-dance-floor friends used to practice dancing at home in the mirror.

I've always avoided this, as I'm afraid to see what's really going on.

Given that I'm going to be getting married to one of "them," people who enjoy dancing and may or may not be good at it, I probably owe it to him to give it a shot.

He's willing to forgo dancing at our wedding, which is very nice, but I know he'd prefer to include it.

(If only people went ice skating at weddings! I would definitely be one of the first people on the ice at my wedding.)

So I guess I'll be struggling to get over my dancing aversion, which I suppose means practicing dancing in front of the mirror. I'd like to apologize in advance to my downstairs neighbors. I don't like this any more than you do.

ooo

No Chips, No Nuts

I tend to think all of us are connected by a sort of fundamental shared humanity, and that conflict arises from misunderstanding and underneath it all, we're more similar than we are different. This is how I generally feel until confronted with some thought or behavior to which I cannot relate at all, something so disturbing, transgressive or aberrant I'm forced to contend with the notion that perhaps we're all really, truly alone.

My fiancé, for example—someone with whom I generally feel a kinship—recently told me that he's vexed by having to eat. Figuring out what to eat and then eating it feels like a chore. He wishes he could just take a pill in the morning containing a full day's nutrients and be done with it. I would rather just kill myself, which is how I feel when I'm dieting, which is pretty much all the time.

Who is this stranger, this animal whose relationship with food is so different from mine? His is akin to the most casual of dating. Mine is more of the hot and heavy sort, passionately on again and off again.

He also sometimes "forgets" to eat and is reminded by the growling of his stomach. I've literally never forgotten to eat. Sometimes I forget *not* to eat. For example, I recently enacted a "no chips, no nuts" rule, as my workplace seems to be filled with bowls of each and a few minutes of mindless grazing can torpedo a day's worth of restraint. Plus, I've had a realization, an epiphany of sorts, that I don't really love nuts. I'm OK with them—cashews in particular—but there are other things on which I'd rather waste calories. I feel the same about avocados and mayonnaise. They just aren't worth it, and if you disagree, you can write a letter.

Anyway, I made this "no chips, no nuts" rule for myself and announced it loudly, which is what I do. Later, my fiancé and I were looking at wedding venues and took a break to regroup at the bar of a hotel. He ordered a something, and I ordered a Diet Coke served in a '50s-style bottle with a 2013-style price. They were both delivered on tiny overly thick napkins along with a silver tray of nuts and olives. "Oh, no! I'm eating nuts!" I exclaimed through a mouthful. I'd completely forgotten about my rule.

On the plus side, it was mostly macadamia nuts that passed my lips. While I've painted all nuts with the "too caloric, not worth it" brush, I will admit that macadamia nuts and the aforementioned cashews are almost worth it. Peanuts are never worth it.

The good thing about marrying someone whose relationship with food is so estranged is that our children might have a fighting chance. For their sake, I hope they inherit his ability to purchase or receive tempting items, bring them into the house and completely forget they exist. I am not this way. At all times, I know exactly where to find all the delicious items in the house. Some people have a good sense of direction; I have a good sense of carbohydrates. I *feel* them. And, like anyone with an ability bordering on psychic, sometimes my gift is distracting.

Now, if you'll excuse me, I'm receiving messages from some pretzels trapped in the cupboard.

ooo

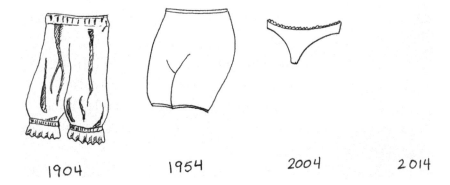

1904   1954   2004   2014

Goodbye, Underpants

As sometimes happens when you play fast and loose with laundry, I recently found myself in the ineluctable position of needing to take my dog for a walk but having no clean underwear. I debated either fishing them from the dryer and making do with soggy drawers or trying to rectify the situation by blowing a pair dry with a hair dryer—which is how you achieve lush, voluminous underwear. In the end, I vetoed both those ideas as far too uncomfortable and time-consuming. Instead, I did what I think any hero in my position would do: pulled on jeans and headed for the door.

What I discovered, which is the same discovery I made the last time this happened, is that I felt free and unencumbered, as if I could have walked for miles without tiring. Is underwear fatigue a thing? Is that what I've experienced every other underwear-wearing day of my life? Because what I thought felt normal no longer feels normal, and I long to be free of these society-mandated undershackles. I have experienced freedom and bliss in the nether regions and don't want to go back.

I know what you're thinking: Perhaps my underwear doesn't fit right, and that's why I am so much more comfortable without it. I can't say whether you're right or wrong (you're wrong), but does anything fit quite so well as nothing? Extensive scientific research—and by that I mean my own experience of going without underwear one and a half times—has led me to think that perhaps humans were not meant to wear a smaller pair of pants under their pants.

Would you wear a glove under a glove? A hat under a hat? A sock under a sock? Whither undergloves, underhats and undersocks? Now, an argument could be made that a sock is actually an undershoe, but look at the sandal. Or the pump. Or any "Miami Vice" episode. There are plenty of sockless shoes and far too few underpantsless pants.

As I say this, I can feel your judgment. "Ladies are meant to wear underwear," you are thinking. "And what's more," you would probably say, "I'm lucky to live in a time when underwear is slight and negligible, as opposed to the days of yore when underwear was the size of a tablecloth and required those same people who brush your teeth with a stick to help you into and out of it."

I'm not sure about the brushing your teeth with a stick thing, but I saw it in a wonderful documentary called "Shakespeare in Love," so I'm pretty sure it's true.

Back in the days of hoop skirts, crinoline, bloomers and stick-based dental hygiene, ladies didn't really do anything other than fan themselves and occasionally fall onto fainting couches. They also sat for portraits and giggled. Again, I'm no historian. But I've seen the paintings. Ridiculously uncomfortable undergarments are fine when your entire to-do list involves reclining. Today's modern woman has a busy schedule of walking the dog, doing laundry, checking Twitter, fishing dog toys out from under the couch, arguing with her fiancé about potential baby names (I'm not pregnant yet, but I am getting a head start on this one, as apparently, it's going to take a lot of ironing out), ironing, driving, working, heating things up in the microwave and having the same conversation repeatedly about the opening credits of "Homeland."

Him: Does Louis Armstrong have something to do with terrorism? What's he doing in here?

Me: I think it's that Carrie likes jazz.

This is all to say there's a lot of movement and bending over and leaning and reaching. And during movement is when underwear likes to strike. The underwear ringleader says: "Now! Go now! Climb up her butt. There's no time to waste!"

This is why I encourage you to try going without underwear for just an hour and see whether it isn't both life-changing and life-affirming.

ooo

I Went to Hooters

I went to Hooters for the first time yesterday, and while I won't be joining the Hoot Club any time soon—an actual club you can join, I have the sign-up sheet and everything—it was less awful than I was expecting. Allow me to explain.

My reaction to finding out I'd be recording a live "Adam Carolla Show" podcast at Hooters, a place I'd heard about and joked about but blissfully never visited, was not good. I tried to act like a sport, but inside I was filled with dread. Imagine a red-blooded American male's reaction to finding out he'd be going to Hooters for work. He'd probably be pretty excited. Now, for contrast, imagine his reaction to hearing he'd have to sit in a room filled with angry women complaining about their periods. My reaction was more akin to the latter. Ever since that Hooters date got put on the calendar, I began acting as if there were a giant Boob of Damocles hanging over my head.

Every time I imagined setting foot in the boob-palace-disguised-as-a-wing-joint-disguised-as-a-sports-bar, every fiber of my being rebelled. When I was told it'd be best if I arrived at least 45 minutes early, I acted as if I'd been asked to let someone remove my kidney with a rusty spoon. While 45 minutes really isn't much time, an extra 45 minutes in a place they can't pay you enough to be in is an eternity.

Part of the discomfort came from trying to pretend I didn't feel this way. I'm a cool chick who can hang with the guys; I'm not some uptight prude! I'm not a square! I'm totally down with ogling hot chicks and, um, dipping sauces. Or whatever it is that happens at Hooters. Plus, I'm a professional. If I get news we're going to be performing in my ex-boyfriend's living room, which, frankly, would be a weird place to do a live show, I would be pleasant and delightful.

Except I was neither. Instead, I was miserable, short-fused and cranky.

But beyond the discomfort of trying to deny a feeling, there was the actual dread of having to go to Hooters, which I'm still trying to sort out.

It didn't make sense to me that I should feel this way—I've got a dirtier mind than a lot of men, and I enjoy a good fart joke. So why was I so uncomfortable? It occurred to me that I'd feel less uncomfortable in an actual strip club. There, at least, we're all being honest about our intentions.

I'm fine with places that cater to baser instincts, just as I'm fine with strip clubs and prostitution. Hell, I think prostitution should be legalized. What it really comes down to is that I'm uncomfortable being looked at through the same lens that people see Hooters waitresses—and, by extension, says the voice in my head, all women who happen to be in Hooters. If you lined up a bunch of Hooters waitresses and then stuck me somewhere in there, it would be like that "Saturday Night Live" sketch in which amid the attractive women there's one who is missing teeth and has a shrunken hand. I'm not saying I'm grotesque. I know I'm not. But in a bar that celebrates an itty-bitty waist and two big things in your face, I'm just different.

My fiancé, who, like almost all men I've talked to, has been to a Hooters before, told me it would be different than I was expecting, that it'd be 99 percent sports bar, 1 percent Hooters waitresses.

Turns out he was right. I was happy to leave, but not for the reasons I expected. We happened to be there on a day when the entire surrounding area was filled with people, traffic was nightmarish, parking was impossible and I couldn't hear myself think.

As for the boobs, though, I was fine with them.

ooo

Say No to This Show

Yesterday, I found myself sitting on my exercise bike, not pedaling, and watching "Say Yes to the Dress" on my iPad with tears streaming down my face.

This is problematic for a number of reasons, not the least of which is I do not like "Say Yes to the Dress."

For the lucky uninitiated, "Say Yes to the Dress" is a horrible reality show that follows unlikable brides and their unlikable families while they choose wedding gowns with the help of unlikeable but sassy wedding consultants.

Every time I've tried to watch it in the past, I've found it wholly uninteresting and hard to follow, and I've wondered why anyone would enjoy watching it since everyone's annoying; it feels contrived; and all the dresses look the same.

But that was before I myself went wedding dress shopping and attained a wedding dress fluency that I'm hoping will go away soon—I suspect it's occupying valuable brain real estate.

A-line, trumpet, mermaid, tulle, organza, drop waist, boning, beadwork, bustles. I worry what's going to happen as we get closer and closer to the wedding because my brain, which feels pretty well-packed to the gills with info on '80s sitcoms and wedding dresses, still needs to accommodate a bunch of information about flowers, chair rentals, cakes and stationary.

Do you have a favorite flower? Do all women? Because recently, in regard to the wedding, I was asked, "What's your favorite flower?" to which I responded, "Uh, pretty ones?"

So I guess I'll be learning the names of flowers now. Who knows what useful stuff my brain will jettison to make room? If I walk down the aisle, spin around three times to the left, drool and then yell "Trumpet! Lemon! Begonia! Fit and flare!" just know that I've been pushed too far.

But back to the show. There are two versions: the original, set in Manhattan, New York, and a spinoff, "Say Yes to the Dress: Atlanta," set in Houston. Just kidding! It's set in Atlanta.

Sort of like the difference between MTV's original "Real World," which followed the lives of seven people thrown together to see what happens when people stop being polite and start being real, and the later versions, which followed the lives of seven wannabe reality stars to see what happens when people stop wearing clothes and start drinking on camera, the difference between the Manhattan and Atlanta shows is awareness. The people in the latter show seem keenly aware they're being filmed—you can imagine a producer saying "Here, say this" moments before they say anything, Either that or the people themselves have learned to speak in uber-sassy sound bites, which is worse.

As for the cloying phrase "Say yes to the dress," I've learned that people actually say this in real life. Bridal consultant after bridal consultant (that's what the salespeople at the bridal salons are called, by the way, as if they're brought in to do a little consulting on the company that is your wedding as opposed to hired by the store to sell you a dress) said to me: "Are we saying yes to the dress? Are we ready to say yes to the dress? Could this be the dress? Could you say yes to this dress?"

It's a weird sort of pressure that kicks in near the very end of your appointment (you have to make an appointment with a consultant, natch), but I found it very distracting because I kept wondering whether the phrase or the name of the show came first. Then I spent a lot of time trying to come up with a spinoff, and all I got was "Say Super to the Grouper," a show about sassy annoying people who wear fish.

I look forward to turning back into the real me, the one who thinks "Say Yes to the Dress" is hard to follow and all the dresses look the same, as opposed to this new bridal version of me who cries while watching the show because so-and-so's grandfather would have loved that drass! (That's how you say "dress" in Atlanta.)

And I look forward to forgetting all the names of the flowers I'm about to learn.

ooo

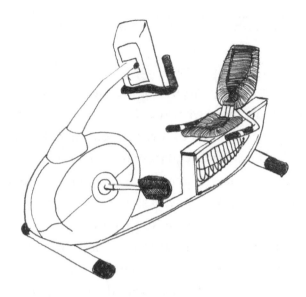

The Exercising Is Not Going Well

I've noticed a disturbing trend of late. The exercise bike I purchased for all the right reasons—to inject some heart-healthy cardiovascular exercise into my day, to help me attain the inner peace and tranquility that comes with regular exercise and because it was on sale—has turned into an expensive and not very comfortable couch. I do not feel good about this. To wit: I recently found myself sitting on it, not pedaling, watching "Say Yes to the Dress" on my iPad with tears streaming down my face.

It hasn't always been this way. When I first got the bike, I'd set the timer for an hour and then ride it for an hour. It was glorious. It went exactly how it was supposed to go. The bike was set up in the living room, and for distraction while riding, I'd watch TV or listen to the radio. Then, in preparation for houseguests arriving, we moved the bike into the office, lest our friends and family get wise to the fact that we're exercising and run out and buy a bike of their own to get in shape faster than us.

I thought I'd hate having the bike in the office because we don't have a TV in the office—whatever would I do to pass the time while riding? But it turned out that I loved it. The proximity to my desk made me feel like I was able to get work done and exercise at the same time. Instead of taking a break from working to commit to a full hour to exercise, as I'd been doing when the bike was in the living room, now I could grab whatever I was planning to peruse at my desk (a quick glance at the action piles here would suggest I was planning to peruse old envelopes with notes scribbled on them, a box of thumbtacks, dog treats, business cards, a photo from a friend's son's "Call of Duty"-themed bar mitzvah, 8,000 Post-it notes, bottle caps, a nail file and an old iPhone case) and instead peruse it on the bike. Now I was really maximizing my productivity! Instead of wasting time at my desk and calling it work, I could waste that same time on the bike and call it work plus exercise. I was beginning to understand why celebrities like Jimmy Kimmel install a treadmill desk in their office.

So that was going swimmingly—the tight buns were nearly in reach, and my fiancé was pretending he wasn't distracted by the reflection in his computer screen of someone in his periphery huffing and puffing and reading envelopes. But then I made an upsetting discovery: I can't think and move at the same time. I'd actually realized this a while ago but forgotten. When I'm walking and talking on my cellphone and someone asks me a question that requires some thought, I have to stand still to answer. It doesn't really bother me, but it does bother the people directly behind me and the people I'm walking with. Well, suddenly, I found myself on the bike, checking my emails and holding still when I'd get one I had to think about. For me, apparently, thought is the enemy of motion. No wonder stupid people love fitness!

But all of this wouldn't be a problem if the timer on the bike kept going whether I was pedaling or not. Then I could just cheat myself of the benefits of exercise and be in and out in an hour. Instead, the bike pauses while I pause, so an hour of exercise takes months.

And this was before I realized the best way to pass time on the bike, and also with friends and family, while watching TV and while conversing, is to play a diabolical game called Candy Crush. Now I hop on the bike, set it for an hour, begin playing Candy Crush and stop pedaling within the first five minutes. If this keeps up, I will spend 2014 trying to complete the hour I set on the bike before Thanksgiving 2013.

I guess the answer is to just set a kitchen timer. Obviously.

ooo

I Do Not Enjoy Baths

A lot of people I know love baths. They find them refreshing, relaxing, rejuvenating, restorative and other words you'd find in an ad for a spa. They're always talking about how there's nothing better than a hot bath, how they can't wait to get in the bath, how they were feeling sore and achy until they took a bath, how the first thing they do in a hotel is take a bath ... bath, bath, bath. I actually have friends who Instagram photos of the baths they're about to take.

The result of all this incessant bath chatter is I feel I'm missing out by hardly ever taking a bath, especially since I live in a home with two giant bathtubs that have turned into awkward, inefficient storage units. The one in the master bathroom is a vast ring of emptiness surrounded by grooming products that don't fit in the small stall shower, candles, unopened bubble bath I received as a gift, dust and hair. The tub in the guest bathroom serves as a ledge for 8 million old issues of Entertainment Weekly and Vanity Fair.

As I do with Grape Nuts—another thing I don't appreciate in the way I think I'm supposed to—every so often, I try to see what all the fuss is about.

"I know! I'll take a bath," I announce to myself. Then I buzz around the bathroom lighting candles and grabbing a bunch of magazines and turning on music and trying various ways of pinning my hair up so it won't get wet. "Look at you, treating yourself right," I'll titter, as if I'm truly in for an afternoon of sweet indulgence. Then I'll finally get into the tub, lean back and let the waves of relaxation wash over me for about 60 to 75 seconds until I'm bored and want to get out.

This is what everyone loves? What am I missing?

Even though my body longs to be on terra firma, I'll force myself to soak for another few minutes because I can't believe I went to all this trouble to create a mood for less than two minutes of sudsy enjoyment. Then I think of all the candles I lit—by this point it's hard not to think of them, as I feel I'm suffocating in a cloud of pomegranate—and imagine the flames somehow jumping from the counter to the roll of toilet paper and igniting. It'd be such a shame if I burned the house down while I was in the tub, although if that were to happen, the tub really would be the right place to be. But the tub has its dangers: Are there any electrical items nearby that could fall in? Did I leave my straightening iron plugged in? Did I turn the stove off? Did I leave a cigarette lit, even though I haven't smoked in 15 years? Where is the dog? What if I'm missing important emails?

By the time I finally allow myself to get out, I realize I haven't even washed myself. As I do that, memories of being a little kid, which is the last time I really took—and didn't enjoy—a bath come flooding back.

After washing, I worry I'm soaking in soapy water and realize I won't feel clean unless I take a shower, which is what I wish I'd done from the beginning. I do not feel relaxed, rejuvenated or refreshed. I feel annoyed and sweaty, and the sum total of my afternoon of sweet indulgence is that I've wasted an hour plus and I'm in bad mood.

Yet, I'm aware that in a few months I will try this again and have the same realizations because I can't seem to break this cycle.

People who love baths: What am I doing wrong?

Same question regarding Grape Nuts.

ooo

It's Time to Start Christmas Shopping!

It's always around this time of year, when Christmas is right around the corner, barreling toward me like a one-horse open sleigh pulled by a drunken Clydesdale with rabies, that I think to myself, "Huh, I should probably do some Christmas shopping."

I do this every year. Each and every year. Each and every single year that I've been alive minus the ones during which I wasn't expected to give anyone gifts because I was too young. When they say youth is wasted on the young, I think that's specifically what they're referring to: gift forgiveness.

And in case you're wondering, I did not just return home from a tour of duty, come up for parole or wake up in a bathtub full of ice with my internal organs removed and a note that told me to go to the hospital. I have no good excuse for waiting this long, other than it's what I do every year. It's my thing. Being completely horrible at time management and in denial of the way annual holidays work, despite tons of evidence to the contrary, is my thing. And on a smaller scale, being in denial of monthly occurrences is also my thing. This is an overshare—consider it a special holiday overshare—but I'm the woman buying feminine products every single month while also thinking: "I should really be buying these ahead of time. It's not as if I wasn't expecting this."

But back to Christmas shopping. Based on the number of stressed-out, irritable people I see at the stores acting as if this holiday was thrust upon us out of the blue, as if we haven't been seeing Christmas decorations since what feels like summer, tons of us are terrible at time management! It's not just *my* thing; it's *our* thing.

Of course, there are exceptions. You might be one of those overachievers who got your shopping done early and are now sipping mulled cider out of a festive seasonal mug, watching "It's a Wonderful Life" and cherishing your loved ones as opposed to resenting them. You're probably also one of those people who wraps gifts really well and folds over all the edges and smoothes the paper and sticks decorative doodads like pine cones and candy canes into the bows. I bet you have a wrapping room or a wrapping closet or at the very least a dedicated spot for all your gift-wrapping items.

I have some gift wrap floating around my car, and when I give someone a present it looks like a cat vomited wrapping paper onto the box and a 3-year-old got into the tape. And somehow I'm always throwing out my back while trying to wrap gifts. I don't know where the correct spot to wrap them is, but I know where it isn't—hunched over in a corner somewhere, on the ground, sweating, hoping no one walks in. Another terrible place to wrap gifts is on your bed, because you're likely to cut right through your bedspread.

Clearly, I need some kind of stand-up craft table. I'm definitely going to add that to my plans for the dream house, which includes an ice skating rink and a salad bar.

I keep hoping that one day I will be one of the organized decorative-doodad-using mulled cider-sipping type-A people, but I just don't know whether I have it in me. I'm too comfortable with being uncomfortable.

Now, if you'll excuse me, I need to hit the mall and then climb under my desk to wrap some gifts.

ooo

The Problem With New Year's

I'm tired of New Year's Eve.

I'm tired of the pressure, the anticipation, the crowds, the expense, the traffic, the countdown, the forced merriment, the ball drop, the yelling and those stupid novelty glasses.

I'm tired of feeling like wherever I am, there's probably something better going on somewhere else.

I'm tired of telling myself that *this year*, I will really do it up; and *this year*, I will make the most of it; and *this year*, I will do something fun and festive with my makeup to indicate that it's New Year's Eve and I am a fun person, and then doing my makeup just like I do every other night, which just seems so ... boring.

Once, in eighth grade, I wore Christmas ornament earrings. They were little pink hollow glass balls, just like ones you'd hang on the tree but smaller and made into earrings. They were

awesome and whimsical, and they sandwiched my face in FUN.
Then one slipped off and shattered on the sidewalk as I was
walking home. I've been trying to attain that level of festivity ever
since. In fact, every time I'm back at my parents' house, I see the
little set of replacement Christmas ornament earrings given to me
many years later in a vain attempt to fill the Christmas ornament
earring-shaped hole in my heart. But it's just not the same, not
only because these are little metallic glittery globes—so much
more garish and obvious than their predecessors—but also
because I'm no longer that girl. Now I'm a combination of
Scrooge before he sees the ghosts, the character in "We Need a
Little Christmas" who needs a little Christmas and the Grinch.
That is to say I'm an adult. Sort of.

But back to my beef with New Year's Eve. By this point, I've
pretty much tried all the permutations. I've gone to giant parties
(too chaotic); I've played board games with friends (too staid);
I've chased doomed love (pathetic); I've pretended I didn't realize
a relationship was on its last legs because, how do you break up
between Christmas and New Year's? (not a good way to usher in
a new year); I've waited until the last minute to make plans
(tough on the people you're making plans with); I've waited until
almost the last minute to make plans (I pretty much always
wait—I'm indecisive!); and I've stayed home and done nothing at
all (liberating but depressing). I've also been between parties at
the stroke of midnight, on the road at the stroke of midnight and
in a bathroom reapplying lip gloss at the stroke of midnight.

The thing is, the older I get, the more I realize that fun
happens when you aren't really setting out to have it, when the
expectation isn't there, when it just creeps up on you and you find
yourself singing at the top of your lungs in a car or laughing
uncontrollably at an offhand comment or doing something you

didn't expect to find yourself doing, such as ice skating. But it's impossible to do anything on New Year's without the expectation of fun. Fun is New Year's raison d'être. Hence, it can't live up to itself.

But if you think just not observing it is an option, it isn't. I tried that, and it wasn't fun, which is why I'm thinking maybe this year I'll wear glittery eyeliner. That sounds festive.

ooo

Is My Dog a Pot Dog?

The new year started in a bit of a panic when, after his evening walk, my dog began throwing up, and then flopped over on his side. I called him into the other room because I wanted to see him move. He popped up, trotted about 10 feet and then stood there looking at me. I was relieved for about a second, but then, he began wobbling and he sat, as if to steady himself. His head was shaking back and forth a little. Then he began throwing up again. In between heaves, he was twitchy— I'm not sure where twitching ends and convulsing begins, but it seemed to my fiancé and me that he was on the border. Definitely south of seizure but north of twitching.

Here is the thing about my dog: He is the cutest, sweetest, most adorable dog in the entire universe, and if anything happens to him, I will die. For this reason, I'm sure something is going to happen to him. It's just science.

So, convinced something awful was happening, we scooped up the little guy, debated whether to put him in his car carrier or in my lap (I finally decided on the carrier for fear that if he was in my lap, he would sense and feed off my anxiety—again, just science), jumped in the car and drove to the vet. I spent the entire car ride swiveled around staring into the metal grate of the pet carrier that was strapped into the back seat. Oliver was reclining against the towel in a way I'd never seen. He was flopped on his side, and his head was leaning on the towel not unlike a drunk passed out near a toilet. I was semi-convinced we were going to lose him on the way to the vet, and it was a small victory every time he held his head up.

Oliver was a runt, 2 ounces when he was born and hand-fed because his mother was a whore. Actually, that's not true. I'm not sure what her deal was, but I know she had better things to do than nurse him, so he was saved and raised by humans. He is a third of the size he's supposed to be—a 6 1/2-pound Cavalier King Charles Spaniel—and he's always skinny no matter how much he eats, the lucky bastard.

But because he's a runt, I'm always worried there's something wrong with him despite being assured from the outset that runts often have a will to live that makes them healthier than their siblings.

When we got to the vet, the nurse took his vitals and told us he was stable. She said the vet was going to examine him and then would be in to see us. We could have a seat in a tiny room filled with posters about heartworm and cat toxins. After what felt like a lifetime but was probably only half an hour (still a long time when you're panicking), the vet came into the little room and asked whether Oliver could have gotten into anything. He said that Oliver seemed like a "pot dog."

Was the vet accusing us of being stoners who leave our pot around the house? I was both offended and kind of happy that I give off a libertine vibe, but I explained that there's no pot in our house. The vet asked whether Oliver might have found a joint on the walk. We admitted that he does put everything in his mouth when he's walking. The vet listed the things that could make him act this way: pot, nicotine (a cigarette butt or nicotine gum), Vicodin, Xanax, alcohol or licking antifreeze. He brought Oliver in so we could see him. He was unsteady on his feet and seemed disoriented. He couldn't walk in a straight line and seemed to only sort of recognize me. "He seems drunk," the vet said.

On the vet's recommendation, we left him overnight while they followed a protocol for toxin ingestion—activated charcoal and IV fluids.

The following day, we picked him up, and he was himself again. If he had any realizations about himself, his place in the universe and the way we're all one while he was tripping, he hasn't shared them with me.

At this point, I view all gum as nicotine gum, which is what I suspect may have been the culprit. Sure enough, during his first walk back in the neighborhood, he tried to put gum in his mouth. He's an addict.

An intervention is in order.

ooo

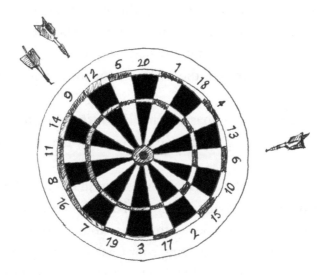

About That Resolution to Be More Punctual

I made three New Year's resolutions this year, and in case you're wondering, yes, I'm the New Year's resolution-making kind. I know plenty of people who refuse, saying they regard the entire year as a chance to work on self-improvement, and making resolutions once a year just sets you up to be disappointed in yourself. However, in the same way I like to make a wish before I blow out my birthday candles even if I know it isn't going to come true—at this point, I highly doubt River Phoenix will ask me out—I like annual rituals.

Here were the three:

–Be more punctual.

–Be better with names.

–Stop trying to change people's minds.

It's the last one that's proving the most difficult, and also the first one. The second isn't vexing me but only because it's early yet, and I haven't met that many new people.

But let's go through them one by one for the next three weeks.

There have been phases of my life during which I've been early and ones during which I've run late. My default is to run late.

Growing up, it was usually a fashion meltdown that delayed me. Shortly before leaving the house I'd look in the mirror, dislike what I saw and feel compelled to try on all the outfits in my closet, march out into the living room, ask my parents whether each successive one looked OK, refuse to believe what they told me and then anxiously put the clothes I started in back on because, by this point, I was significantly late.

"Don't you need to go? Aren't you late? What time were you supposed to be there?" my mom would ask worriedly in the midst of the neurotic fashion show. "A half-hour ago," I'd say somewhat angrily through tears, as if this was beside the point. The point was that I didn't look good, and I certainly didn't feel OK, and seemingly, no one got it in the way I needed.

I want to think this was a normal teenage-girl thing, but maybe it was specific to me. It's a shame I was raised by humans instead of therapists.

Things got better in college, probably because I had fewer full-length mirrors.

Eventually, I moved to New York where, miraculously, I became the person who was usually a little early. It was something about not driving and instead relying on public transportation—getting anywhere in New York pretty much takes about an hour—that forced me into a lifestyle of stopping cutting it so close. There were a small handful of times where I did run late, but there is something deeply unpleasant about nervously wondering while sitting in the back of a cab, waiting on a subway platform or running down a busy block when you're going to arrive, more so than when you're behind the wheel of your own car. I never wanted to experience it again.

The punctuality stayed with me for a good while upon moving back to California. But in the three years since I've been back, it's been slowly eroding. It's no longer about how I look—though that particular meltdown is always within reach—but rather a combination of having a puppy I feel guilty about leaving and working with Adam Carolla.

Adam famously views time as money on a very literal level and therefore regards every extra minute he spends getting somewhere early as diluting the amount he's making. Because I often ride with him to shows, I've become accustomed to stepping on stage a couple minutes after arriving. It isn't his thinking that's rubbed off on me so much as a comfort level with cutting it very close.

So this year, I'm trying to revert to the earlier, more punctual version of myself if only because every time I'm five or 10 minutes late these days—which is every time I try to go somewhere—I feel surprised and confused. Clearly, my calculations are off. And I feel weird and ashamed of the way the last 45 text messages I've sent have been a combination of "Almost there!" and "A couple mins away!" and "Sorry, almost there, a couple mins away!" Sometimes I think I should just text if I'm going to be on time.

Since making the resolution, I've been better but not perfect. If you're also grappling with trying to be more punctual, how are you going about it? Let me know, but don't expect me to remember your name.

ooo

I Can't Remember Your Name

The second of the three New Year's resolutions I made this year—the first being to be more punctual and the third being to stop trying to change people's minds—is to be better with names. It's hugely upsetting to me that I even have to make this resolution. Allow me to explain.

I've always had a very good memory. It's something I pride myself on. I'm the kind of person who can remember the details of something you told me ages ago, something you don't even remember having mentioned, like who took you to get your ears pierced (Aunt Judy), what you called your childhood stuffed animal (Zippy the Monkey) or the name and occupation of your high school ex-girlfriend's ex-boyfriend (Doug; frozen yogurt).

People are always saying: "I can't believe you remember that! *How* do you remember that? *I* barely remember that!"

I don't know. I just do. It's like a parlor trick. If you tell it to me, I will remember it. I won't remember streets or directions or where I put my keys, but I will remember trivial details about things that have zero impact on our daily lives. It's just my gift.

Except lately, it isn't.

Lately, I go to pull a name and the wrong one comes out. "Oh, yes. Steve!" I'll announce. "Or Mark? Wait. No. Frank?" It's dispiriting. And sadly, it's been happening with increasing frequency. It's as if my brain is an overstuffed bookshelf and I can't grab a book without a few extras tumbling out. I'm losing my edge.

And don't even get me started on the shame I felt when I tried to make a reference to the actress who played Pippa on "The Facts of Life"—Sherrie Krenn (now Sherrie Austin)—and what came out was Sherilyn Fenn. It's inexcusable!

But perhaps the worst part of all this is that lately, when someone tells me his or her name, it doesn't even go in. My brain doesn't even try to store the info. I will meet a group of people, shake their hands and hear their names, but it's as if they're on mute, as if I've been slipped a long-acting roofie that only kicks in when I hear a name.

And a second later, when someone asks me the name of that person because I am so good with names, I literally have no idea. I didn't hear it the first time. And because I'm now aware that I've quickly gone from great with names to terrible with names, I'm afraid to use anyone's name for fear of getting burned. Even when I'm pretty sure I know—because the person just told me or because I actually know this person and we have met repeatedly—I still try to avoid it because I just don't trust myself anymore. It may sound like nothing, but it feels like something, and it's awful.

I know there are all sorts of tricks to remembering people's names—mnemonic devices and picturing their names written on their foreheads and the like. Not only do I have trouble remembering names but I also have trouble remembering to remember names. I should write it on my hand.

The part that's so upsetting is I know how important people's names are to them. When someone forgets your name or calls you by the wrong name, it feels like a betrayal. Like perhaps you misjudged them, or misjudged how they saw you because it turns out they didn't see you at all.

Except I do see you. I just don't know what to call you. Suddenly, those nametags that I always rolled my eyes at don't seem like such a bad idea after all.

ooo

I'm Not Trying to Change Your Mind

O ver the last couple weeks, I wrote about my New Year's resolutions to be more punctual and better with names. Those are going pretty well. I've been arriving to work with a few minutes to spare, and I can still rattle off the names of the people I met at a meeting last week: Sarah, JR and Brandon. Kevin? Well, two out of three isn't bad. It's my third resolution, to stop trying to change people's minds, that's proving the most challenging.

I like to be understood. I can't feel an emotion without attempting to put it into words, can't have an experience without translating it and can't negotiate a confusing situation without trying to figure it out. When there's a gap between what I'm feeling and what I'm saying, or when I sense a gap between what someone else is feeling and what they're saying, I find it agonizing. I'm like an emotional accountant—which, by the way, would be the worst kind of accountant. Never get your taxes done by an emotional accountant. I need everything to be reconciled.

When I say I'm trying to stop trying to change people's minds, I don't mean it entirely in a literal sense. If someone likes a color I don't like—orange, let's say, which always reminds me of the '70s and makes me feel hot and nauseated—I will not try to convince that person of the superiority of colors in the cool spectrum. Go ahead and like awful colors. More blues and greens and purples for me. Or if someone likes a band I don't care for, I am fine with it so long as we aren't taking a road trip. Or if someone insists that "House of Cards" is good, as everyone insists, and I disagree because Kevin Spacey's Foghorn Leghorn accent drives me insane and because, my God, the show couldn't be more boring, then so be it.

But if people listen to my podcast, on which I talk openly about what I'm experiencing, and they take issue with how I approach a problem, or worse, with the fact I'm choosing to speak openly about the problem, or even with the fact I have an audience at all, I feel compelled to try to change their mind. "They must just not understand what I'm saying," I think. They didn't hear me correctly; they just didn't get it. And then I fantasize about explaining and re-explaining and finding the precise words that would get these people to change their opinions about me, to reserve judgment of me, to *like* me.

This is not a useful compulsion. All that energy spent trying to get people to change their minds could be put toward something much more rewarding and effective. It shouldn't really matter so much what someone thinks of me. In this scenario, I am the color orange. People have a right to like and dislike whatever they want.

Trying not to change people's minds is also about learning to trust boundaries.

I was talking to my dad the other day. My dad is one of those people—perhaps you have them in your family—who is always angry at a handful of people. Instead of trying to defend these targets from his, to my mind, irrational ire, I attempted to let him vent and to not change his opinion because in the end, what does it really hurt that an old man somewhere is angry at someone who will never find out? Why must I correct my dad? Why is it so important that he feels about people and the world exactly how I feel about them and it? And who is it helping when I try to make him see things my way?

If I can really pull this off, really stop trying to change people's minds, I predict it will free up a lot of mental energy to remember people's names.

ooo

What I Wish They Told Me About Planning a Wedding

Before planning a wedding, a process I'm in the midst of, I never understood what the big deal was. I never understood why people talked about it like it was one of the big stresses of life, why untold numbers of books had been written about it, why blocks of programming were devoted to it and why it took people I love and made them unrecognizable. I also never understood the halting wide-eyed warnings people would issue when I told them I was planning a wedding. "Whatever you do," they would say, grabbing my wrist for emphasis, "Don't read the bridal magazines. They will just drive you crazy. Read two, but then stop." Or "Don't listen to all the voices. Just remember, it's about what you and Daniel want." I also received the exact opposite advice, people saying, "The sooner you recognize that a wedding is for your family and really isn't for you and Daniel, the easier it'll be."

The intensity and variety of the advice I received made me think I wasn't taking the whole endeavor seriously enough—not that I wasn't taking matrimony seriously because I was—but that somehow I wasn't taking wedding planning seriously enough. For example, I hadn't signed up for ballroom dancing classes, started a scrapbook or even made a profile on Pinterest. And when people discovered this, and that I was trying to plan the thing in about four months, they gave me a look that was a mix of pity, fear and vicarious thrill, probably the same look I would get if they found out I was going on a lengthy polar expedition and all I brought to sustain me was a cardigan, half a Fresca and a peanut.

"But what could possibly take so long?" I wondered. "Why do people start planning 14 months in advance?"

Now I know, having almost come out the other side of it. And here's what I wish people had explained to me.

If you are the kind of person who looks at two vendors online and then chooses one and is happy with that decision and never looks back, you don't need an impossibly long lead time. However, the planning process takes a long time if you're a relatively thorough person who likes to make sure each decision is the best one, given a number of factors, from quality of service to cost.

I'm indecisive, and I like to weigh my options. To feel comfortable, I like to thoroughly vet each detail—something I should have known about myself to begin with but didn't quite recognize—and so, I'm finding the process to be immensely stressful and time-consuming.

Another thing no one really warned me about: the paralyzing effect of "IT'S YOUR DAY!" You will receive this message saying that your wedding is your big day and you should love every aspect of it between two and three million times in the course of planning a wedding. You will think it isn't really affecting you, but then you will sit down and try to choose between two florists. One uses peonies, and you aren't sure whether you like peonies, and on the one hand does it really matter—a flower is a flower—but on the other hand, IT'S YOUR BIG DAY and you should love everything about it, which is a lot of pressure.

At a certain point, you will wonder why you're doing this. It's stressful and expensive, and you will think you should elope or postpone the wedding or just not get married at all. And you will freak out. And then you will discover the parallel universe of wedding websites and books devoted to this reaction. I don't know if it's a generational thing or just something that has always happened but wasn't often talked about, but women getting cold feet isn't that uncommon, especially women who get married in their 30s and are used to being independent and fear the loss of that identity.

At the outset, I thought of planning a wedding as akin to planning a party, something I don't have a lot of experience doing, but how hard can it be? Now I realize it's about coming to terms with what it means to be married. And figuring out whether you like peonies.

ooo

I'm Not Moody (and Other Lies)

I'm beginning to worry that I've been lying to myself for years about my fundamental nature. I don't mean in the big ways—it's not as if I used to think I am a writer named Alison who owns a puppy and is about to get married but recently discovered that deep down I'm a retired black man named Fred who lives for recreational chess. But in terms of the nuances of personality, I'm no longer sure.

For example, I don't think of myself as a moody person. I think of myself as a good-natured even-keeled person who's been in a bad mood on and off for the last 30-something years. I was puzzling over this recently, about the fact that for someone who doesn't consider herself moody, I sure am moody. And then I began to wonder why it is I cling to this notion when most evidence is to the contrary.

I think it's that in college, which apparently is the last time I revisited myself, I wasn't moody. For whatever reason, college really was four great, enlightening, fulfilling and enriching years. Everything else has been a little less thrilling, a fact I kind of hate to acknowledge. I don't want to be that person for whom college was the best four years, though I'd rather be that person than the one for whom high school was the best four years—that person was a cheerleader.

The problem with those school-was-the-best people is that they peaked years ago. I want to peak shortly before I die. Or perhaps live in a sustained state of peaking. I just don't want the best to be behind me.

Let me ask you this: Do nonmoody people sometimes feel like crying for no reason at all? Do nonmoody people wake up and think, "I just have to get through the day, and then I can go back to sleep?" Do nonmoody people only answer their phone 0.5 percent of the time? I realize what I'm describing sounds like low-level depression, which probably goes hand in hand with moodiness and hence doesn't apply to me.

And then I was thinking about the other ways in which I might not be who I say I am. For instance, I hardly ever listen to my favorite band. If someone were to ask me who my favorite bands are, I would have to reach far back into the memory reserves, as the first thing to go with age is the ability to keep up with current music. But the name I always throw out there, Sunny Day Real Estate, is a defunct group I hardly ever listen to because the music is too beautiful and too poignant, the same reasons why I love it and why I can't listen to it. So should it really be my go-to favorite? In the same way that unromantic people say you marry the person you're dating at the time you're ready to get married, that it's more about timing than anything else, your favorite band is probably the band you're listening to at the age it's important to declare a favorite. And don't even get me started on favorite movies. At one point, in grade school, I used to consider "Ruthless People" and "Big Business" to be my favorites.

This is what I think: There's who you want to be, who you are and who you let yourself become. I want to be a stylish skirt and dress person, but I'm actually a bootcut jeans person who lets herself be a sweatpants person at home.

But I'm not moody.

ooo

Just Me or Everyone?

On my podcast, "Alison Rosen Is Your New Best Friend," I do a segment called "Just Me or Everyone?" during which people write in and tell me things they think or do that make them wonder if it's just them.

The idea for the segment came when I was out walking one day in Brooklyn, where I lived at the time, and a fire truck tore down the street, engine blaring. "I wonder if it's headed to my apartment," I thought, imagining my house in flames because I'd left my straightening iron on. It was a familiar thought, the same one I had every time I was out walking and heard a fire engine's siren. Then I wondered whether I was the only one who had this thought. (I'm not, but it's less common than I would have expected.)

I've been doing the segment for a few years now, previously on a live-streaming internet talk show I did from my living room in Brooklyn and now on my twice-weekly audio podcast. And as such, I have a pretty good sense of the idiosyncratic thoughts and habits we all share. I thought I'd reveal some recent submissions (people tweet them to me at @ariynbf, my show's Twitter handle) along with my comments, lest you also do these things and think you're the only one.

@abelopez "[I] get super nervous and tongue tied when I call someone expecting a voicemail and they answer."

Yes! Sadly, I tend to prefer avoiding the phone altogether these days. But when I'm reveling in the comfort of thinking I won't have to connect with another human being and then suddenly I'm confronted with a live one, it's scary. Side note: how sad that's it come to this.

@LarryAugsberger "Is it just me or does everyone stare at the rug when they're on the toilet and cross their eyes a little until they see little faces in the pile."

I stare at the floor tiles. Only some kind of maniac would have carpet in his or her bathroom, unless you're referring to a bath rug. In that case, I get what you're saying, but I recommend the dimples in the tiles. Better for shapes but still not as good as asbestos-filled cottage cheese ceilings.

@Mike Chamernik "If someone mispronounces my name and asks if that's how you say it I say 'You got it.'"

I definitely don't do this. Maybe I should?

@thomaschad "[I] feel like a dish u hand scrub w tons of soap and hot water is not as clean as 1 that is just stuck in washer and prob gets a squirt of h2o."

Yes! I thought this was just me, but I have a hang-up about dishes that are hand-washed. I'm convinced I can taste the soap. No amount of water is enough to rinse it off.

@higherbassist "when someone doesn't respond to a text message in a timely manner I begin to worry about their well-being."

Yes! Or I begin to worry they're mad at me. And yet, I take my sweet time responding to people. I'm a jerk.

@keenandion "I love the warm cozy feeling of a gas station on a dark stormy morning."

I love dark stormy mornings, but I would hardly describe gas stations as warm and cozy. In my experience, they're usually cold and smelly.

@thompsona2006 "Whenever I hear a 100 (percent) money back guarantee, I wonder if the company sends the returned item out to their next customer."

Well, I never worried about this before ... but now I will. So, thanks?

ooo

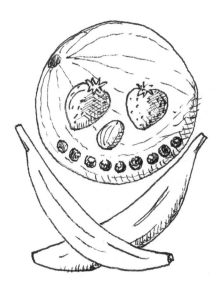

Goodbye, Fruit Salad

I've never been a particularly coordinated person. I frequently find myself banging my arm or shoulder on door frames I've passed through hundreds of times, tripping over familiar coffee tables, dribbling soda down my shirt and trying to close the trunk of my car and walking away only to hear it pop open. But I usually manage to get through my day without significant incident.

Then yesterday happened.

I was in Las Vegas to perform a show at Treasure Island. Adam Carolla and I flew in with just enough time for him to go to his signing and for me to go to my room, put on makeup and change clothes before the show. On a day when I'm performing, I'll drink coffee up until the time I go on. Except for a recent show in Chicago during which I had to leave the stage to pee, an ordeal that still haunts me because the feeling I experienced before exiting the stage was one of such extreme discomfort I couldn't focus on anything else, it always works out fine. That is except for the part where I can't get to sleep that night and I chalk it up to not sleeping well in hotels, as opposed to the 14 cups of coffee I drank earlier. But a ritual is a ritual.

So after arriving in Vegas, checking in and doing this thing I do when I first get to a hotel room where I pace around in tight circles trying to figure out what to do first (Unzip my suitcase? Hang up my coat? Check my email? Charge my phone? Turn on the TV? Open the curtain? Close the curtain?), I began to get ready. This involves a lot of walking back and forth between the bathroom, where I'm putting on makeup, and the bedroom, where my suitcase is. At one point, when my makeup was on enough for me to begin drinking coffee, I waltzed out of the bathroom, tripped over the carpet, ricocheted off the dresser, bounced off the bed and landed dazed near the desk. Next, I tried to pour some milk from a glass into the coffee. Why is it impossible to do this move without spilling everywhere? You never appreciate the pour spout until you're trying to pour milk into your coffee from a glass and it goes everywhere. It would have been easier if I'd poured the milk directly into my fist and then thrown it in the direction of the cup.

Then I distractedly took a bite of fruit salad—not a regular part of the ritual, I should add—and all hell broke loose. As I chomped down, I somehow managed to snag a bit of cheek between a molar and a grape, and my lower lip between another grape and a tooth, and I drew blood in multiple spots. It was like someone else's teeth were inside my mouth, attacking me. How does this happen? It's not as if this is the first bite of food I've had since I got my adult teeth. Presumably, I've been doing this thing where I put food in my mouth via spoon or fork, chew it up and then swallow it thousands of times. Why did this one time cause such wanton destruction? Why the multiple grape-cheek-tooth pileup? I want to blame the grapes. Had they not been there, I don't think this would have happened. But had I not been overly ambitious thinking I could handle a bite involving more than one grape plus cantaloupe, I probably would have been fine. But does everyone else know that more than one grape equals danger? It's like being trapped in a small closet stuffed with a bunch of balloons and a knife. Sounds like a scene from an awful horror movie that I would never watch.

In sum, my mouth hurts still hurts; I can't sleep; and I'll never attempt to eat fruit salad again.

ooo

About the Book

For my birthday a few years ago, my husband presented me with a hand-bound book of my columns from the first year I was syndicated. At the top of each one was an illustration he'd done, having worked late into the night at his office to keep it a surprise.

Daniel told me he made it because he wanted me to know he believed in me and felt I should be published in book form. Also, I gave him an over-the-cabinet-door organizer as a gift one year, and he wanted me to relive his look of disappointment and confusion every single day for the rest of my life. (He didn't say this, but it was implied.)

The fact that this gift from him to me has now been turned into a real book, one that you all can hold in your hands or read on your screen, makes me so happy.

Below is the original cover he made and the copyright page.

The book you're reading is very much the same as the original gift, just printed by a slightly larger press in a slightly larger run.

Alison Rosen
the syndicated columns:
year one

Acknowledgments

Thank you, Jack Newcombe, for reaching out to me and suggesting I write the column that became this book.

Thank you, Alissa Stevens, for seeing this through, and working patiently and diligently around my schedule.

Thank you, Simone Slykhous and everyone at Creators, for working with me on the column.

Thank you, Will Swaim and everyone at OC Weekly, for helping me become a better writer. I miss you all.

Thank you to all the other magazines and newspapers I've worked at or been published in.

Thank you to my parents for loving and supporting me.

Thank you, Diane Meyer.

Thank you, Laura, David, Max, Josh, Beth, Emily, Claire, Nick, Cyndi, Hennessey, Cody and Sam.

Thank you to all my friends in Costa Mesa and New York.

In no particular order, thank you, Trevor Stockinger, Tom Rapp, Jeff Fox, Jenna Kim Jones, Allan Moss, Greg Heller, Greg Fitzsimmons, The Angoras, Yami Burns, Roya Young, Dustin Goot, Anthony Mattero, Shane Dawson, Todd Christopher, Itay Reiss, Jana Marimpietri, Alyssa Reuben, Adam Nettler, Bellamie Blackstone, "The Facts of Life," Refreshe sodas, Hillary, Meghan Parkansky, Lisa Lawrie, Leeann Ward, Rafael Castañeda, Josh Holtsclaw, Jason Dix, Becki McClure, Diane Cross, Elizaveta Ramnarine, Racquel Michel, Alexis Chen, Ulysses Adkins, Lisa Robles, Jessica Trevino, Diana Dow, Sarah Ellis, Jessica McMickle, Reenee Ray, Vanessa Rose, Lisa Nero, Kevin Portillo, Tony Lokey, Amanda Dix, Cassy Bedell, Leila C Rollins-Cohen, Sheila Brown, Britta Harris, Rebecca Cook, Shannon Kenney, Stephanie Plummer, Shannon Stokes, Candace, Moe, Eric

Pasquale, all the Patreon supporters and #AlisonPeople, "Best Friend's Fancast" and "JMOE Patrol," the listeners and guests of my podcast, who make me feel less alone, my friends in the podcast community, Steve Wilson, David and Nina Raphael, Ellen, Elaine, Carrie Wambach, Grace Wakagawa, "The Adam Carolla Show," "Red Eye" and "Today in New York." I know I am forgetting people!

Thank you, Daniel, Oliver, Wendy and Elliot. You are my heart.

About the Author

Alison Rosen is a writer, TV personality and podcaster best known for her podcast, "Alison Rosen Is Your New Best Friend," which has over 25 million downloads, as well as being the former "newsgirl" and co-host of "The Adam Carolla Show."

Alison's roots are in traditional media: She began her career as a professional journalist early, scoring a contributing writer byline for the Los Angeles Times while still in high school. Her work has appeared in Rolling Stone, People, Seventeen, Elle, the New York Post, Vibe, Spin, Maxim, the Village Voice, The Huffington Post, OC Weekly, Time Out New York, Yahoo and Bon Appetit, among others.

Alison has built a loyal following through her blogs, videos, social media and interactive Ustream show (the precursor to her podcast), for which she was dubbed "the future of television" by former AOL CEO Barry Schuler.

She has also carved a niche for herself as a pretty, comical, slightly devilish TV personality.

Years ago, she played in a band, which she likes to mention because it sounds cool. And she was born in Oakland, which she believes gives her cred even though she only lived there for seven months.

Alison currently resides in Los Angeles with her husband, baby and dog. She always gets lost, even though she has GPS.

TROPICAL ATTIRE ENCOURAGED
(AND OTHER PHRASES THAT SCARE ME)
is also available as an e-book
for Kindle, Amazon Fire, iPad, Nook and Android e-readers,
and as an audiobook.
Visit creatorspublishing.com to learn more.

∘ ∘ ∘

CREATORS PUBLISHING

We find compelling storytellers and
help them craft their narrative,
distributing their novels and collections
worldwide.

∘ ∘ ∘

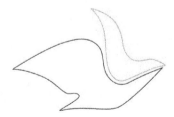